THE LEGEND OF
STANLEY

150 Years of The Stanley Works

For Dad ... with a full measure of love.

Also by Jeff Rodengen

The Legend of Chris-Craft	*The Legend of Honeywell*	*The Legend of Applied Materials*
IRON FIST: *The Lives of Carl Kiekhaefer*	*The Legend of Dr Pepper/Seven-Up*	*The Legend of York International*
Evinrude-Johnson and The Legend of OMC	*The Legend of Briggs & Stratton*	*The Legend of Amdahl*
	The Legend of Ingersoll-Rand	Run with it: *The Legend of AMD*
Serving The Silent Service: The Legend of Electric Boat	*The Legend of Halliburton*	*The MicroAge Way*

Publisher's Cataloging in Publication
Prepared by Quality Books Inc.

Rodengen, Jeffrey L.
   The legend of Stanley : 150 years of the Stanley works / Jeffrey
L. Rodengen.
   p. cm.
   Includes bibliographical references and index.
   ISBN 0-945903-13-8

1. Stanley Works Inc.   2. Tools—United States.   3. Hardware
industry—United States.   I. Title

TJ1195.R64 1996   338.7'6219'08
                                   QBI96-20244

Write Stuff Syndicate, Inc.

1515 Southeast 4th Avenue • Fort Lauderdale, FL 33316
1-800-900-Book (1-800-900-2665) • (305) 462-6657

Library of Congress Catalog Card Number 95-060795
ISBN 0-945903-13-8

Completely produced in the United States of America

10 9 8 7 6 5 4 3 2 1

TABLE OF CONTENTS

INTRODUCTION

MANY GENERATIONS OF craftsmen and hobbyists have relied on Stanley products at one time or another. A young entrepreneur reaches for Stanley hammers, paintbrushes, levels and rulers to convert a spare bedroom into a home office. Weekend hobbyists use Stanley planes, scrapers, chisels and saws to build sun porches, doll houses and swing sets. Professional contractors and mechanics rely on the quality and wide variety of Stanley tools millions of times every hour.

Even those who don't use tools regularly rely on Stanley products in more ways than they realize. The hinges, locks and bolts on their doors are probably made by Stanley, as are the automatic doors at the supermarket and shopping mall. The Stanley Works also manufactures the most popular lines of mirrors, closet organizers, doors, gates, garage door openers, fastening equipment, mechanics tools, hydraulic tools and air tools.

Today, The Stanley Works is a sophisticated multibillion-dollar global organization. But the company began in a rather modest way, in a one-story wooden building purchased in 1843 by Frederick T. Stanley and his younger brother,

William. Despite the small scale of the operation, The Stanley Bolt Manufactory quickly gained a reputation for quality and value. The business grew steadily, and by 1852, the brothers decided to incorporate another business, named The Stanley Works. Five years later, The Stanley Works acquired The Stanley Bolt Manufactory, and the combined companies continued to grow through product ingenuity and a legendary commitment to quality and service.

While The Stanley Works flourished, another New Britain company, led by Frederick's distant cousin, Henry Stanley, also enjoyed an excellent reputation. The Stanley Rule & Level Company, founded in 1857, had established the industry standard for attractive, versatile and reliable rules, levels, planes, and related tools. In 1920, the two companies merged, and the Tools Division of The Stanley Works was established. The legendary Tools Division has produced some of the most innovative, practical and enduring tools ever made, including the Bailey plane, the Powerlock rule, and the Surform shaper.

The Stanley Works has grown up with America, literally helping to build the homes, shopping centers and offices of our nation. Stanley hinges are on the World Trade Center and other important buildings.

Ever since the Civil War, the company has proudly contributed, when necessary, to wartime production. In World War I, The Stanley Works manufactured gas-mask components, belt buckles and automatic rifle magazine tubes. During World War II, the company contributed steel, tools, gas-mask parts, and much more.

The long history and outstanding reputation of The Stanley Works have attracted a substantial number of collectors, who sometimes pay thousands of dollars for antique Stanley tools. Tool collector clubs and auctions have sprung up throughout the nation, and newsletters are distributed across the continent, brimming with questions and information about recent discoveries.

Through more than 150 years of growth and innovation, The Stanley Works has never abandoned the principles established by Frederick Stanley — providing value for customers, treating people with respect, acting with integrity and providing quality products.

Frederick Stanley found time in his busy schedule to take an active role in his community. When New Britain became an independent town in 1850, he was named warden. Together with six burgesses, he organized the first town government. He also headed up the committee that planned New Britain's first water supply system, and became mayor of New Britain when it became a city in 1871.

Frederick Stanley established a standard of community service that has remained a model for The Stanley Works. Today, the company generously contributes tools, funds and volunteer hours to many charitable organizations, including Habitat for Humanity, the home-building initiative often made visible by former President Jimmy Carter, seen wielding a Stanley hammer on the television news. The Stanley Works generously supports the Special Olympics, the March of Dimes, the United Way, and other worthwhile programs. It improves education through scholarships, donations, and social leadership. The company has contributed tools and funds to disaster relief around the world. Concerned about the environment, The Stanley Works has set aside hundreds of acres for preservation, and even constructed a fish ladder to help migrating salmon swim up the Farmington River to their spawning grounds.

While other manufacturing companies have closed down or moved out of New Britain, The Stanley Works has remained. Employees know that they are valued, and they respond with an uncommon dedication and loyalty. In the company lunch rooms, it's often possible to find three generations of a New Britain family sharing a table.

The Stanley Works has proven that good deeds and sound business decisions can go hand in hand. Under the leadership of CEO Richard H. Ayers, The Stanley Works is now in the midst of an ambitious plan called *Four by Four*, which seeks to grow the company to $4 billion by 1999, while reducing operating costs and assets by $400 million. The company already has the distinction of returning more consecutive dividends than any other industrial company on the New York Stock Exchange.

Of course, the man or woman who uses Stanley hammers and saws to build a bookcase probably isn't thinking about the company's long history. They just know that Stanley helps them do things right.

THE STANLEY RULE OF LIFE

THE STANLEY WORKS, among the most recognized names in American industry, has acquired a true institutional status. I know, for Stanley actually attained an even higher, nearly mystical quality in the household of my youth.

My father, Marvin Rodengen, worked at the St. Paul, Minnesota assembly plant of the Ford Motor Company for over 30 years. As a maintenance engineer with a specialty in sheet metal engineering, Dad was a consummate tool user who had the uncanny ability to fix just about anything that required repair throughout the sprawling auto factory.

Since the use of tools was central to Dad's life, and supported our family of five, it's not surprising that his passion for repair and precision tools would spill over into his leisure time as well. My older brother, Jim, my sister, Judy, and I, each learned that using the proper tool for a specific task was essential, lest we risk the fury of the sovereign of the tool cabinet. More indelible, though, was our indoctrination into what we came to understand as The Stanley Rule of Life.

It was a somewhat metaphysical connection between tool and the cosmos when, one day, Dad methodically extended his six-foot Stanley zig zag folding rule, and carefully laid it out on the workbench.

"See this," Dad mused, pointing to the beginning of the ruler. "This is where you are born. And here," he would point, after running his finger slowly down the full length of the extended ruler, ending at the 72-inch mark, "Here is where you die."

He would calmly quote the consensus of 1950s-era scientists, who had determined that the average life span for a man was 72 years of age. Even this information, thrust into the consciousness of my 9-year-old psyche, was a revelation that would cause me to stare at the speckled ceiling of my bedroom in the middle of the night for weeks.

"Here's where I am today." Dad would search for his current age, and then plant his often-soiled finger on the corresponding inch-mark along the Stanley ruler. The first time he explained this unique philosophy, he had progressed to about the 31-inch mark, approaching the all-important halfway mark of the ruler.

"You see this," Dad would say with perceptible anguish, running his finger from the 32-inch mark back to zero. "This is all gone now, finished, just a memory." Then, with a hint of hope and enthusiasm as he approached his conclusion, he would slide his finger from the 32-inch mark to the other end, resting at 72 inches for effect. "This is all that's left, my son," he would say in a quiet voice. "This is what I have left."

Then, taking his finger and laying it at the 9-inch mark, he would say, "Now, this is where you are. This is what you've done, and this is what you have left of your life. You'd better make every inch count, because they turn into feet and yards before you know it."

With that, Dad would pick up the common ruler, which moments before had somehow been transformed into an icon of nearly biblical propor-tion, rivaling such other legendary tools as the scepter of Moses or the fabled Ark of the Covenant.

At about ten-year intervals, he would unfold the timeworn ruler on the workbench and repeat The Stanley Rule of Life, changing only the loca-tion of his fingers, gradually inching his way toward the inevitable 72-inch mark.

Last year, as Dad approached the 72-inch mark and the end of the ruler, it was obvious to his family that he was depressed. I scoured the hardware stores until I found an eight-foot zig zag rule to send him for his birthday. Now, when he unfolds the ruler, he can look forward to the possibility of 96 inches, an attainable goal if he can maintain his health as well as he does his tools.

In fact, I'm looking forward to sending him the ten-footer one day.

ACKNOWLEDGMENTS

RESEARCHING, writing and publishing *The Legend of Stanley: 150 Years of The Stanley Works* would not have been possible without the cooperation and assistance of many people.

The development of historical time-lines and a large portion of the principal archival research was accomplished by my valued and resourceful research assistant, Torrey Kim. Her thoughtful and careful investigation into the early years of The Stanley Works has made it possible to publish much new and fascinating information on the origins and evolution of this unique organization.

The candid insights of Stanley executives, both current and retired, were of particular importance to this project. I am especially grateful to Richard H. Ayers, chairman and chief executive officer, and R. Alan Hunter, president and chief operating officer, of The Stanley Works. Both executives generously gave many hours of their valuable time to this project.

Donald Davis, former chairman and chief executive officer of The Stanley Works, also devoted many hours to this project, sharing his insights from many years of association with The Stanley Works.

Particular gratitude is extended to Richard C. Hastings, Hoyt C. Pease, John S. Parsons, Jonathan B. Scott, and Ronald Gilrain, former Stanley employees who shared their many experiences and memories with me. The enthusiasm of tool collectors, including John and Randa Walter, and Walter W. and Charles H. Jacob, was a welcome inspiration.

Critical insights on The Stanley Works were provided by Richard Huck, vice president of finance and chief financial officer; John Turpin, vice president of operations; C. Stewart Gentsch, president and general manager of Stanley Tools Worldwide; Joseph L. Jones, president of Stanley Tools North America; Thomas Jones, president and general manager of Stanley Access Technologies; Henning Kornbrekke, president and general manager of Stanley Hardware; Patrick Egan, president of Engineered Components; Robert Hudson, director of marketing for Stanley Tools Latin America; John Francis, president of Hand Tools for Australia and New Zealand; Charles Blossom, president of Mac Tools; Wayne

King, president of Stanley-Proto Industrial Tools; Dick Dandurand, president and general manager of Stanley Door Systems; Thomas E. Mahoney, president and general manager of Stanley Customer Support; Patricia McLean, manager of corporate communications; Donna N. Alexander, manager of marketing communications; Francis Zambrello, manager of the Eagle Square Plant; and Carl Stoutenberg, product line engineer manager for Hand Tools.

Gratitude is also extended to Parker A. Thompson, senior marketing manager of Access Technologies; Cindy A. Martins, marketing manager of Stanley Hydraulic Tools; Mary Ellen Leary, marketing manager of Stanley Home Decor Worldwide; Beverly Demianenko, marketing secretary of Stanley Door Systems; Gregory Furdas, marketing analyst for Stanley Hardware; Tibor T. Egervary, marketing communications manager for Stanley Storage Systems; Lynne Duncan, administrative assistant for Mechanics Tools; Sharon Morgan, advertising manager for Stanley-Proto Industrial Tools; and Carol Meola, catalog development manager for Stanley Mail Media Companies.

Cheerful assistance was provided by Linda Lundie, administrative assistant for Richard Ayers and Alan Hunter; Rachel Long, executive secretary for Richard Huck; Loraine Williams, secretary for C. Stewart Gentsch; Cheryl B. Farmer, contributions and community affairs administrator for The Stanley Works; Fred Elia, director of administrative services for The Stanley Works; Arlene Palmer, of the Local History Room at the New Britain Public Library; and Horace B. Van Dorn of the New Britain Industrial Museum.

A debt of gratitude is also owed to Robert Keith Leavitt, author of *Foundations for the Future, The History of The Stanley Works*, privately published in 1951. His careful research provided valuable details and essential historic verification for this project.

Finally, a very special word of thanks to the staff at Write Stuff Syndicate, Inc., especially Executive Assistant Bonnie Bratton, Creative Director Kyle Newton, Graphic Designer Anne Boeckh, Executive Editor Karen Nitkin, Project Coordinator Karine N. Rodengen, Marketing and Sales Manager Martha Lord, Logistics Specialists Joe Kenny and Rafael Santiago, Production Managers Sharon Khan and Ray Mancuso, Proofreaders Bryan Henry and Cathy Ritter, and Office Mascot Kodak Rodengen.

The bustling Main Street of New Britain, Connecticut, in the 1890s. The Stanley Works, founded in New Britain in 1843, remains headquartered in this New England city today. (Photograph courtesy of the Local History Room, New Britain Public Library.)

CHAPTER ONE

FREDERICK T. STANLEY

*"The secret of this company's success is an open one. All who will
may avail themselves of it, and all who do so will succeed. One word
tells it all, and that one word is — Excellence."*

*— Asher & Adam's Pictorial Album
of American Industry, 1877*[1]

FREDERICK T. STANLEY was born in 1802, when there were 16 stars on the American flag and Thomas Jefferson was the third president of the United States. The young nation was growing at a rapid pace. The cotton gin, invented by Eli Whitney in 1793, was creating an economic boom in the South, requiring increasing numbers of slaves to harvest the valuable crop. The Louisiana Purchase, which would double the land holdings of the United States, was still a year in the future.

In 1802, New Britain, Connecticut, had fewer than 1,000 residents and was not even officially considered a town. But the parish, located 15 miles west of Hartford, bustled with several small manufacturing businesses, including two brass foundries, one of which made "bells, andirons, clocks, spoons, harness and shoe buckles."[2] Blacksmiths and tinsmiths were also well-represented in New Britain.

The items manufactured in New Britain generally had to be portable enough to be transported by horsecart over the narrow roads and rickety bridges in use throughout New England. Odell Shepard, Pulitzer Prize winner and former lieutenant governor of Connecticut, wrote about the vendors of these wares, known as Yankee peddlers, in his 1937 biography of Bronson Alcott, the renowned educator and philosopher who lived from 1799 to 1888.

"They went South and West and even 'way down East,' carrying in handbags, valises, carts, and wagons and everything portable that they thought might sell. They carried news from the seaboard towns into faraway farmsteads and huddles of huts whither, without their help, it would never have come. They carried last year's fashions, public opinions of a decade gone by, and the prejudices that never die out, together with assorted heartbreak for many an uplandish maiden. One fears that they were not always well-bred or perfectly well-behaved. They could not shave often. Their baths were mostly those that they took perforce while fording unbridged streams. Country dogs regarded them with strong and well-founded dislike."[3]

Yankee peddlers were laden with cutlery, kitchenware, cheap jewelry, fabrics, laces, hats, shoes, drugs, books, clocks, firearms and builder's hardware, such as locks, doorknobs, bolts and hinges. "His New England speech and ways caused a good deal of amusement in non-Yankee country."[4]

Above: A bolt of wrought iron manufactured by F.T. Stanley Company, one of Frederick Stanley's earliest ventures, which operated between 1832 and 1835.

Frederick T. Stanley established Stanley's Bolt Manufactory in 1843 and incorporated The Stanley Works in 1852. Among his many civic contributions, he served as the first warden of New Britain.

Frederick T. Stanley

The northeast corner of New Britain was dominated by the large Stanley family and its prosperous businesses, which included a brass foundry, a cooperage and a hat shop. Known as The Stanley Quarter, this was the part of town where Frederick Trent Stanley was born August 12, 1802, to Gad and Chloe (Andrews) Stanley.[5] Even within a family known for Yankee drive and ingenuity, Frederick would stand out. In 1843, he would start a business in a one-story wooden building, which would later be incorporated into The Stanley Works. He would also be elected the first mayor of New Britain, and he would help the community gain rail service, gas lighting and a reservoir-fed water supply.[6]

Frederick Stanley's grandfather, Colonel Gad Stanley, had distinguished himself in the Revolutionary War for his bravery at the Battle of Long Island.

"Captain Stanley was present in the Battle of Long Island, August 27, 1776. It was a disastrous day for the American troops, all of whom were raw recruits, while their enemy were the disciplined troops of England and Germany. Captain Stanley maintained his position as long as it was possible, and at last, when the retreat was ordered, succeeded, by a masterly maneu-

1823 – Frederick Stanley starts a business in Fayetteville, North Carolina.

1829 – Stanley invests in a general store and F.A. Hart & Company.

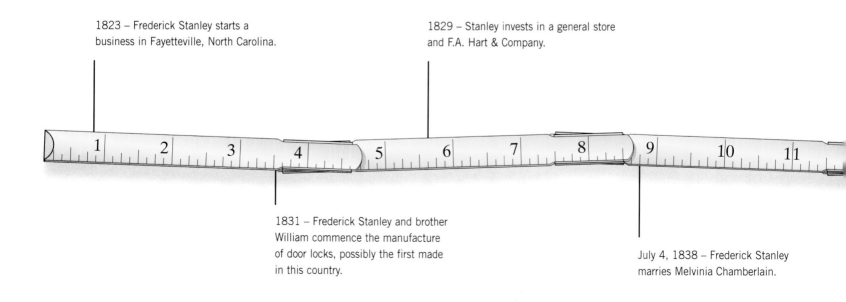

1831 – Frederick Stanley and brother William commence the manufacture of door locks, possibly the first made in this country.

July 4, 1838 – Frederick Stanley marries Melvinia Chamberlain.

Frederick Stanley sold his wares in 1823 from a cart similar to this one.

1843 – Frederick and William Stanley establish Stanley's Bolt Manufactory.

1850 – Frederick Stanley is elected the first warden of New Britain.

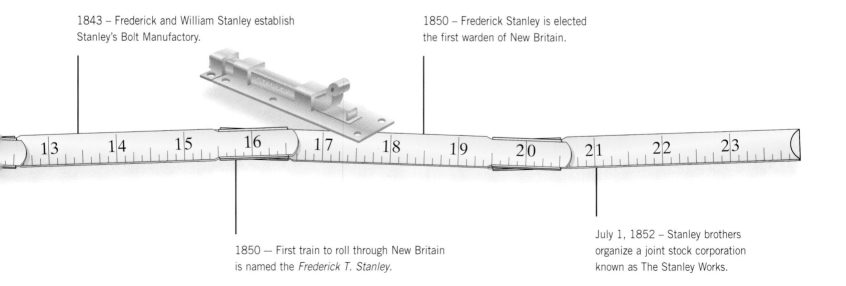

1850 –- First train to roll through New Britain is named the *Frederick T. Stanley*.

July 1, 1852 – Stanley brothers organize a joint stock corporation known as The Stanley Works.

STANLEY'S BOLT MANUFACTORY offered an incredible variety of bolts for securing doors, barrels, chests and shutters. Handles were designed for chests, trunks, windows, and even coffins.

Constructed of brass or wrought iron, the bolts and handles were both attractive and functional. All the bolts featured a sliding and locking construction. They varied greatly in size and strength, from tiny 3-inch barrel bolts to sturdy 60-inch New York City Sunk Flush Bolts. An 1870 catalog notes, "We are the originators of Cast Iron Door Bolts, and maintain the same weight and finish that we commenced with about thirty years ago."

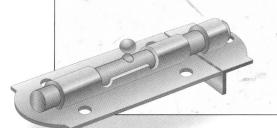

Steam Power

The Stanley brothers were determined to modernize their business beyond any in New Britain, and in 1830, they took the bold initiative of purchasing a steam engine. It was the first steam engine in New Britain, and perhaps in Connecticut. Though the steam engine had been invented in 1712, it was still considered something of a novelty. Most shops in New Britain were powered by either treadmills or water wheels located along the town brook. The largest factories relied on oxen or horsepower. The smallest companies still used "treadle power, worked by the operator's foot."[19]

"Into this primitive situation the Stanley brothers brought a single-cylinder, horizontal, non-condensing, *high-pressure steam engine which they bought from the firm of William Burdon in Brooklyn, New York. It came by water up the river, of course, and had to be hauled, with Heaven knows what creaking of ox-carts, over the country roads to New Britain."[20]*

In 1831, aided by the steam engine, the Stanley brothers began manufacturing the first house trimmings and door locks in the United States.[21]

Stanley Woodruff & Company

Within four years, the brothers were doing so well that they decided to invest in another business. They joined with two brothers named Woodruff who ran a brass foundry, and with a man named Emanuel Russell who had moved to New Britain following a successful career as a retail merchant in New York. The five men were able to assemble the substantial sum of $18,000 in capital to establish Stanley Woodruff & Company, makers of locks. The group purchased a four-story brick building, which later came to be known as The New Britain Lock Factory, and which also housed the Stanley brothers' original business.[22]

William Stanley and the Woodruffs withdrew from Stanley Woodruff & Company in 1838, and Emanuel Russell transferred his share of the business to his son, Henry. Henry Russell and Frederick Stanley took on another partner named Cornelius Erwin, and the firm became Stanley, Russell & Company. The following year, Frederick Stanley withdrew and the firm became Russell & Erwin, which later became the American Hardware Corporation, though the brand names Corbin and Russwin still survive.[23]

Leaving New Britain

On July 4, 1838, Frederick Stanley married Melvinia Chamberlain, the daughter of Samuel C. and Anna (Conklin) Chamberlain, of Sandisfield, Massachusetts.[24] In 1840, the couple moved to Mississippi, where there was strong demand for New England goods. Though no details have survived of this Mississippi period, which lasted two years, it is known that the couple returned to New Britain with ample capital to invest.

Frederick and Melvinia had three sons, Alfred Hubert, Frederick Henry and William Chamberlain, before Melvinia, only 28 years old, died of scarlet fever in August 1843. The two youngest sons, Frederick and William, died within a year of their mother's death.[25] Frederick Sr. moved into a brick house with his younger brother, William, a bachelor, and the two brothers lived there together for the remainder of their years.[26] The only surviving son, Alfred, never worked for The Stanley Works.

Stanley's Bolt Manufactory

The Stanley brothers were heavily involved in the lock business, but they wanted to utilize the steam engine they still owned. They decided to manufacture wrought-iron bolts and handles for doors and chests. In 1843, the brothers purchased a small, one-story wooden building which had been an armory during the War of 1812. Though not yet known as The Stanley Works, the company was born at this site. The Stanleys built an addition to house the steam engine, and Stanley's Bolt Manufactory was opened for business.

"In a short time, the demand for goods was such that additional buildings were occupied, new machinery specially adapted to this work was employed, and the products of the manufactory were soon introduced into the principal cities."[27]

A Model Citizen

Canal, river and railroad development were making available new methods of shipping throughout the country. In 1843, the stagecoach from New Britain to Hartford ran three times a week and cost a quarter,[28] and the following year a new railroad

Frederick and William Stanley purchased the former armory in 1843. After building an addition to house their steam engine, Stanley's Bolt Manufactory was established.

linked Hartford to Boston and New Haven. In 1848 the New York-to-New Haven railroad line was established.[29] Though New Britain merchants could ship from the Newington Station on the Hartford-New Haven line, citizens of the town, led by Frederick Stanley, felt that they deserved their own "steam car" station. In 1850, New Britain was finally connected to the railroad system, and the first locomotive to roll through New Britain was named the *Frederick T. Stanley*.[30]

Even though he worked tirelessly to gain the railroad station, Frederick apparently didn't like trains. He once told the *New Britain Herald* that he wouldn't go near one "for fear the plaguey (sic) thing would explode." However, he eventually overcame his apprehension and rode on the train bearing his name.[31] Also in 1850, New Britain outgrew its rank as a parish of the town of Berlin, and became a town. Not surprisingly, Frederick T. Stanley was elected the first warden. Twenty-one years later, when New Britain became a city, Stanley was elected the first mayor.

The Stanley Works

Stanley's Bolt Manufactory was doing so well that the brothers again made plans for expansion. In 1852, a building across the street, known as The Knob Furnace, went up for sale. The Stanley brothers purchased the building for $4,000, but they were reluctant to risk all their resources in one concern.[32] They instead elected to pool their funds with those of other investors to form a corporation, a process which, at that time, required a special act of the state legislature. With the approval of the legislature, the Stanley brothers organized a joint stock corporation on July 1, 1852, known as The Stanley Works, and separate from Stanley's Bolt Manufactory.[33]

The company was incorporated for the function of "Casting, Forging, Combining and Manufacturing various kinds of Metals, finishing and converting the

A map of New Britain in 1851, the year after it officially became a town.

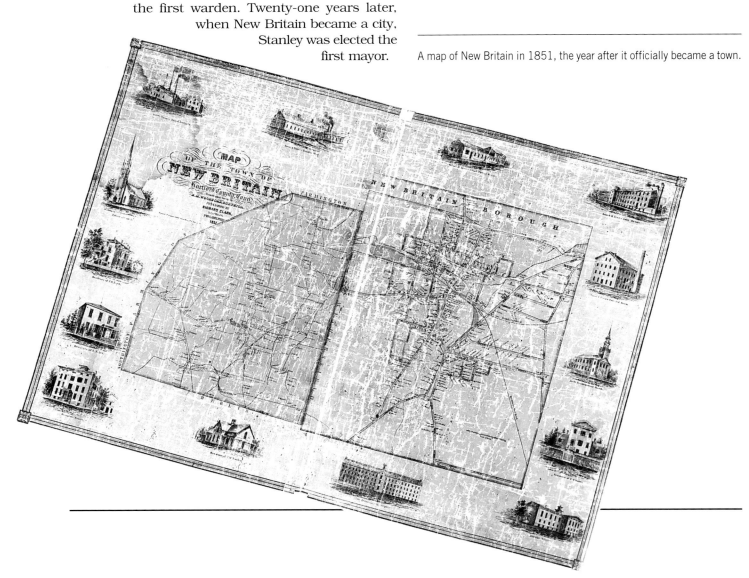

Left: A Stanley price list of 1855, showing hinges as the company's primary product.

Below: An illustration of strap hinges.

same into various articles of Hardware for sale, such as Hinges, Butts, Bolts, Bars, Hasps, Hooks, Staples, Turnbuckles, Rings, Chains and various other articles of Hardware; and to sell and deal in the same."[34]

With Frederick and William Stanley as the principal investors, five other parties purchased shares of The Stanley Works, representing an initial capital investment of $30,000. One of the investors was 22-year-old Walter Stanley, the son of Henry Stanley and a distant relative of Frederick and William. Henry Stanley had purchased 100 shares of the new corporation, at $2,500 a share, in his son's name, with the stipulation that Walter would become secretary and treasurer of the business, and serve as general business manager of The Stanley Works.[35] Since William disliked office work, and Frederick was busy creating the Gas Light Company, established in 1855, and developing the town water works, which brought the first running water to New Britain in 1857, the brothers accepted the arrangement.[36] Frederick Stanley was named president, and Walter H. Stanley became secretary and treasurer.

At the start of operations, the investors contributed only 25 percent of the money they had pledged. This was increased to 50 percent following the first year of operation, and before the end of 1853, another 25 percent of stockholder commitments was required.[37]

In its first year, The Stanley Works sold $7,328 of merchandise and recorded a loss of $361.72.[38]

By February 1854, the stockholders reluctantly voted to put forward the remainder of their monetary pledges. Given the company's tentative performance, "they decided they had better do something radical about the management of their business. Young Walter Stanley very evidently *wasn't*, after all, the man to build it." [39]

Sold by NATHAN PECKHAM, Stationer, 16 State Street, Hartford,

To all People to whom these Presents shall come: Greeting,

Know Ye, THAT I Frederick T Stanley of the Town of New Britain, County of Hartford and State of Connecticut, for the consideration of Five thousand Dollars, received to my full satisfaction of The Stanley Works a Corporation organized under the statutes of this State and so called and doing business in said New Britain

Do give, grant, bargain, sell and confirm unto the said Stanley Works all that certain parcel of land situated in the Town and Borough of New Britain and described as follows, viz: Commencing at the North west corner of My Barn on the Corner of High and Lake St., running Easterly on the line of Lake St. 106 feet, thence Southerly on a line parallel with High St. 110 feet, thence Westerly on a line parallel with Lake St. 106 feet to High St., thence Northerly on the line of High St. to the place of beginning; Containing one fourth of one acre more or less with Buildings standing thereon

To Have and to Hold, the above granted and bargained premises, with the appurtenances thereof, unto them the said grantees their heirs and assigns forever, to them and their own proper use and behoof. And also I the said grantor do for myself my heirs executors and administrators, covenant with the said grantees their heirs and assigns, that at and until the ensealing of these presents I am well seized of the premises as a good indefeasible estate in Fee Simple, and have good right to bargain and sell the same in manner and form as is above written; and that the same is free from all incumbrances whatsoever.

And Furthermore, I the said grantor do by these presents bind my self and my heirs forever to WARRANT and DEFEND the above granted and bargained premises to them the said grantees their heirs and assigns against all claims and demands whatsoever.

In witness whereof. I have hereunto set my hand and seal this 4th day of Sept in the year of our Lord one thousand eight hundred and sixty six

Signed, sealed, and delivered in presence of

Frederick T. Stanley [L. S.]

Chas E Mitchell

John Scanlon

State of Connecticut, County of Hartford ss. New Britain Sept 4th A. D. 1866

PERSONALLY APPEARED Frederick T Stanley his signer and sealer of the foregoing instrument, and acknowledged the same to be his free act and deed, before me

Chas E Mitchell Justice of the Peace.

Warrantee deed of $5,000 from Frederick T. Stanley to buy additional land for The Stanley Works.

CHAPTER TWO

WILLIAM HART

"William Hart was a one-interest man. Unlike Frederick T. Stanley and others of the early New Britain type, he didn't hold with putting his eggs in numerous baskets; he wanted them all in one, right under his own watchful eye. To him The Stanley Works was work and hobby, care and thrill. ... It was his whole thought, night and day."

— Historian Robert Leavitt, 1951[1]

IN MARCH 1854, Frederick Stanley and C.B. Erwin, a stockholder and director of the Stanley Works, asked a 19-year-old assistant station master named William H. Hart to work at the fledgling company. "It was, as events turned out, the most fortunate single thing any of the management of The Stanley Works ever did in upward of a hundred years."[2]

William Hart was born in New Britain on July 25, 1834 to George and Elizabeth (Booth) Hart. His father was New Britain's first village stage driver, becoming manager of the new depot in 1850 when Frederick Stanley helped bring the railroad to New Britain.[3] William started working as assistant station master and freight agent while he was still in high school. In a 1918 interview with *Hardware Age* magazine, he reminisced about this early phase of his career.

"It kept me out of mischief and gave me a solid foundation for a business life. ... I was a clerk for the Hartford, Providence & Fishkill Railway. I sold the first tickets for the first passenger train that rolled into New Britain. It was on January 1, 1850, and as I think of it, it seems but yesterday, although the smokestacks of those old wood burners flared sharply to their huge tops, and the passenger coaches were fashioned after the highway coaches of the day. Checking way bills doesn't

sound like much of a job, but it gave me a knowledge of transportation which at many points in my career as a manufacturer actually saved the day. I often think I might have failed without it."[4]

When Hart joined The Stanley Works, he was engaged to a woman by the name of Martha Peck, and "not quite sure it was time to start raising a beard."[5] Though young, he worked with such enthusiasm and skill that the directors accepted the resignation of Walter Stanley on May 16, 1854, and voted unanimously to make William Hart treasurer and secretary.[6] The Stanley Works employed 25 people at that time.[7]

Frederick Stanley remained president of The Stanley Works, but most of his time was occupied by his original business, Stanley's Bolt Manufactory, and on civic affairs. William Stanley ran the mechanical side of The Stanley Works, leaving William Hart responsible for most other duties. Among his responsibilities were the tasks of maintaining the corporation's accounts and handling all correspondence. He also served as a one-man sales force, traveling to New York, Boston,

Above: Stanley's Bolt Manufactory in 1854.

This photograph of William H. Hart was most likely taken shortly after he was hired by The Stanley Works in 1854. Though he was only 19, Hart quickly made his mark on the company.

Philadelphia, Albany and other centers of brisk wholesale activity to sell Stanley products.[8] In a letter to his son, Walter, in 1919, Hart wrote about his duties.

"While in town, I spent one or two hours a day making rough boxes, laying out and packing goods; an average of about four hours a day in the manufacturing department; and the balance of my ten hours a day attending to correspondence, invoicing and bookkeeping. During busy seasons of the year, I frequently worked with a gang of six or eight men from the factory for two or three hours in the evening, laying out, packing, nailing, hooping and weighing cases, ready for shipment in the morning. I handled the truck, and laid out nearly all of the goods for the gang of workmen to pack. I nailed covers on boxes, then marked them, and with a helper, hooped and weighed them."[9]

Hart's hard work apparently paid off, because in 1854, The Stanley Works nearly tripled sales, recording a profit of $655.57.[10] In 1855, company profits more than tripled again, to $2,200, and the stockholders voiced their confidence in Hart by electing him a director.[11] The stockholders, who were entitled to 9 percent of the profit, elected to return their dividends to the company.

March 1854 – William Hart begins his career at The Stanley Works.

1859 – William B. Stanley resigns and in 1860 Hart assumes general management of the company.

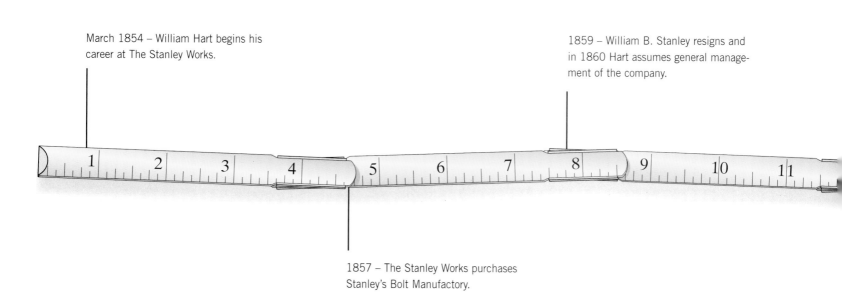

1857 – The Stanley Works purchases Stanley's Bolt Manufactory.

Fine-Tuning Operations

Although The Stanley Works was profitable, Hart realized that the company could do even better. His efforts at trimming expenses, which bordered on the obsessive, probably annoyed William Stanley, described by Leavitt as "a crusty man and one entirely absorbed in the mechanical end of the business, at which he was an expert."[12] Hart ultimately convinced William Stanley of the value of cost-cutting by promising to pay the company out of his own pocket if any money was lost in the process.[13]

Hart told a *Hardware Age* reporter in 1918 that, "Perfect harmony can be maintained only when the shortening of operation carries with it mutual advantages to the workmen and the producers."[14] Hart described his method for achieving this harmony in a 1919 letter to family members.

"I kept an exact account of the number of hours spent by each workman, in the manufacture of each lot of goods, on each operation, from

The earliest Stanley price list, showing all the products manufactured by Stanley's Bolt Manufactory in 1854. Frederick Stanley's earlier company was purchased by The Stanley Works three years later.

1866 – Directors approve $75,000 to build a three-story factory.

1866 – Thomas Tracy is hired to design machines for The Stanley Works.

1870 – Expansion continues with the purchase of land next to the railroad.

the opening of the iron to delivery of the finished articles to the shipping room. I then computed the exact cost of each separate operation required for the production of one hundred dozen pairs of hinges. I was greatly surprised to find so great a difference between one operation and another.[15]

This analysis yielded concrete results, and Hart managed to reduce the cost of producing a standard quantity of hinges from $10 to $4.[16] He was so money-conscious that he had no office help for six years, except for one office errand boy. He even paid $22 out of his own pocket to purchase the desk for his office.[17]

D Company, 1st. Reg., C. N. G.   Field Day, May 11, 1881
Main Street, New Britain, Conn.

Consolidation and Growth

In 1857, The Stanley Works purchased The Bolt Manufactory, combining Frederick Stanley's two businesses in a move that dramatically improved the fortunes of The Stanley Works. "Our business really began to expand vigorously in 1857, when we bought out the door-bolt business of Frederick T. Stanley," Hart told *Hardware Age* in 1918.[18]

But the expansion was accompanied by financial difficulties. In 1858, after dispensing several loans to The Stanley Works, one of Connecticut's largest banks refused to give the company another loan. The general manager named two manufacturers and one merchant who had failed, and warned Hart that, "The Stanley Works' turn will come next."[19] Many years later, Hart reflected on those difficult days.

"I have spent many sleepless nights, retiring without knowing what could be done the following day to prevent our notes from going to protest, which in those days, if repeated a few times, meant bankruptcy. I have probably more than a hundred times started at Mark Moore's at the top of Dublin Hill and walked down the length of Main Street, stopping at 15 to 20 stores, borrowing money at one-third of the places named; then two or three days later, taking the same trip, stopping at the stores where I had previously borrowed money and paying the loans with money borrowed on this trip."[20]

Perhaps frustrated by these difficulties, William B. Stanley resigned in 1859. In recognition of Hart's dedication and drive, Frederick Stanley in 1860 allowed him to "assume the general management of all departments of the company, except with an occasional caution against spending the company's money for new machinery, and the purchase of large quantities of material."[21] According to a company history published in 1951, Hart was completely devoted to The Stanley Works.

Above: A troop of soldiers in New Britain, Connecticut, in 1881. (Photograph courtesy of the Local History Room, New Britain Public Library.)

"William Hart was a one-interest man. Unlike Frederick T. Stanley and others of the early New Britain type, he didn't hold with putting his eggs in numerous baskets; he wanted them all in one, right under his own watchful eye. To him The Stanley Works was work and hobby, care and thrill ... it was his whole thought, night and day."[22]

Hart described to colleagues how he would wake up in the middle of the night with his heart pounding, having been jarred from sleep by an idea for improving The Stanley Works. To make sure he remembered these nocturnal inspirations, Hart tied a knot in his handkerchief and threw it on the bedroom floor as a reminder.[23]

The Civil War

The Civil War began on April 12, 1861, when a South Carolina rebel fired at Fort Sumter, and ended April 9, 1865, when General Robert E. Lee surrendered to General Ulysses S. Grant at Appomattox, Virginia. Between those two landmark dates were four excruciating years of bitterness, destruction and bloodshed. At least 500,000 people perished in battle, and hundreds of thousands more were maimed during the horrible conflict. The physical devastation, animosity, poverty and illness lingered well past the official end of the War Between the States.

The Stanley Works was eager to contribute to the Union cause, and in 1861, it purchased a $10 license to manufacture during the war. "Things were different in those days," Hart later said. "It didn't cost so much to make war."[24] The company made hardware for the army, including hinges, hasps, staples and chest handles.[25] Hart found a way to save floor space, bought more machinery, and managed to double output.[26] During the war, Frederick T. Stanley wrote several thoughtful letters about the conflict that was tearing apart the nation.

"Slavery, it seems to me, is necessarily destroyed by demoralization. Whatever may be the result of this conflict, I cannot believe that any police or military power can hereafter keep them in subjugation any considerable time. It would have been desirable to have emancipation commenced and carried out in a reign of peace."[27]

In another letter, Frederick Stanley asked a friend fighting in the South for his opinion of slavery. "As you now see slavery before you, I want you to point out the course of duty to be pursued toward them and to ourselves and to Humanity. ... Did you learn that they all, or generally, have a longing for freedom, or is it only a small proportion of those generally uneasy while the much larger portion are contented and cling affectionately to their masters? Or do you find that they would desire freedom if they could remain there and not move north or elsewhere? I ask these questions because you have an opportunity for judgement by your invasion and contact with them under favorable circumstances for judging."[28]

Fierce Competition

When the war ended, The Stanley Works found itself embroiled in a different kind of war, as it fought for survival against four major competitors. "They were all bigger than Stanley, all situated close to cheap supplies of iron, all well-established with the trade, and all — so it seemed to Hart — inspired by the devil to sell at outrageously low prices."[29]

One competitor was Lewis, Oliver & Phillips of Pittsburgh, which had recently purchased an iron-rolling mill to add strap and T-hinges to its already comprehensive line. Located at the head of the Ohio River, the company was able to serve the entire Mississippi Valley region. The second competitor was Gilmore & Company, based in North Easton, Massachusetts, and situated among several iron furnaces and rolling mills. This company sold hinges at cheaper prices than Stanley could manage.[30] Third was the Wheeling Hinge Company of Wheeling, West Virginia, also nestled among a number of iron producers, and situated at the headwaters of an inland market still largely supplied by water transportation.[31]

But Roy & Company, of Troy, New York, was the competitor that concerned Hart the most. Hart later spoke to *Hardware Age* about Roy's geographical advantage.

"Roy & Company had a factory within 100 feet of the west bank of the Hudson River, and a branch of the Erie Canal less than 200 feet from their shipping room door, receiving their supply of iron and shipping their goods at a cost not

exceeding 75 cents per ton. ... Our iron was shipped from the Burden Iron Works at Troy, New York, to New York City by water, carted across the city of New York to the wharf of the Hartford Steamboat Company, freighted to Hartford, carted across the city of Hartford, transported by steam cars to New Britain and carted to our factory.[32]

Besides an excellent location, Roy & Company was able to beat Stanley's prices because it spent less money on labor. The company employed boys and girls at 50 to 60 cents per day for 12-hour shifts, while The Stanley Works employed more men than children and worked them only 10 hours a day.[33]

A combination of ingenuity and hard work on the part of The Stanley Works allowed it to prevail over its immediate competition. As Hart later said, "After a hard struggle and severe fighting against fearful odds for several years, one after another of the four competitors were obliged to give up their business."[34]

As part of his effort to combat his competition, Hart introduced new products. In 1866, he determined that The Stanley Works should manufacture wrought butts, since his rivals were having great success selling this style of heavy door hinge, manufactured out of wrought iron. Hart believed that a more efficient manufacturing process, aided by the very latest technological advances, could help The Stanley Works lower the cost of the hinges. He hired Thomas Tracy, the inventor of machines that made hooks and eyes for North, Stanley & Company, as well as knitting machines for the New Britain Knitting Company. Tracy immediately began designing machines for The Stanley Works, as historian Robert Leavitt explained.

This hole-punching machine, invented by Thomas Tracy, was one of the many devices he introduced after he was hired by The Stanley Works in 1866.

"He was an instinctive engineer, not a technically trained one. He never made a drawing if he could help it; he preferred to think out even intricate machines in his head. Such drawings as he made were often traced in chalk on the machinist's bench or on slabs of the raw metal itself. Nevertheless, his machines were not only ingenious, but sturdy. ... For many years, elaborate machines he designed and built were the chief reliance of The Stanley Works for producing hinges with less work — and consequently at much lower cost — than competitors could manage."[35]

One such machine drove pins into hinges, giving The Stanley Works an advantage over Roy & Company, which was still driving pins by hand.[36] In a 1915 interview, Hart explained how the machine gave The Stanley Works an edge over its competition.

"We punched from five to fifteen holes at one operation, and countersunk five to fifteen holes at one operation, against our competitors' punching one hole at a time and countersinking one hole at a time. We swaged the ends of hinges in power presses at one-tenth the cost by the old-fashioned method. We were the first among our competitors to drive pins in hinges by machinery; the first to rivet heads of pins by machinery, the cost of these operations being not more than one-tenth of our original cost and competitor's costs."[37]

To house the large machines designed by Tracy, the directors in 1866 approved capitalization of $75,000 to build a three-story factory on the site of the old one-story wooden building that was the original home of The Stanley Works. In 1867, the capitalization was increased to $100,000, and Hart moved the bolt and handle business from The Bolt Manufactory to the new building. He then moved the wrought butt manufacturing machinery to The Bolt Manufactory and used Stanley's original steam engine to power the butt-manufacturing equipment.

But the company still needed more room to produce enough products to rival the sales of its competitors. Consequently, in 1870, the stockholders voted to further increase capitalization to $200,000, allowing Hart to purchase a triangle of land bounded by Myrtle Street, Curtis Street and the railroad.[38] The land was composed of separate properties that Hart had to negotiate individually; one of the properties was offered to The Stanley Works for $3,000, and included "one acre of land, together with a house and barn, several tons of hay and a heifer." Unwilling to meet the combined asking price, Hart purchased the land for $1,700, and five years later bought the house and barn for $900.[39] Strong sales prompted Hart to request even more space, and the stockholders increased capitalization once again, this time to $260,000.[40]

Hart later told *Hardware Age* that, "In locating machinery in our new factory in 1871, where I could set the machinery in regular order of operation, the actual labor cost of making hinges was reduced fully 25 percent."[41]

The competing companies one by one accepted defeat. The Stanley Works had triumphed over early competitors, and was in a position to dramatically increase both production capability and variety of offerings.

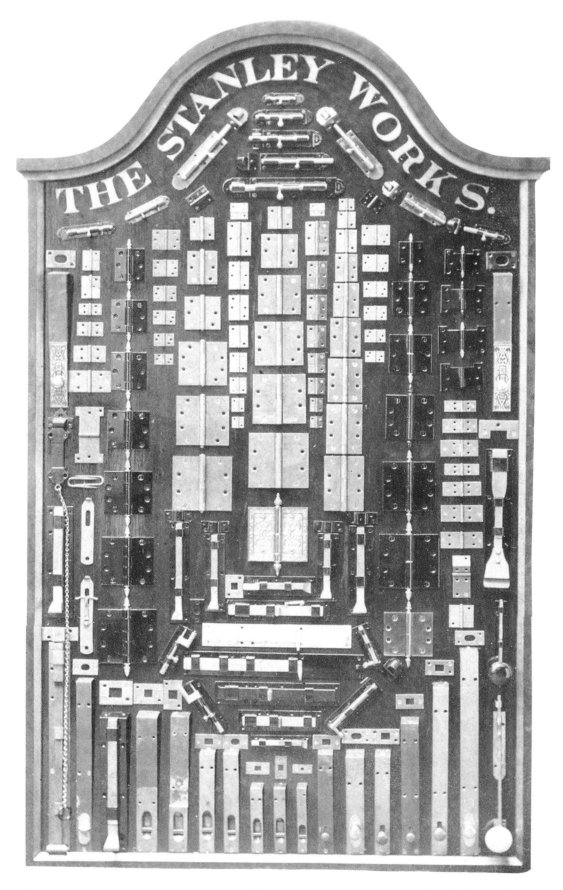

This display board showcases the wide variety of hinges and door accessories produced by The Stanley Works in the 1880s.

CHAPTER THREE

NEW AND IMPROVED

"With my own hands, I operated that machinery and cold-rolled the Swedish iron, which started that day to revolutionize our business."

— William Hart, 1918[1]

ILLIAM HART WAS always searching for ways to improve The Stanley Works. Though the company had triumphed over its immediate competition, Hart wanted to make the heavy door hinges manufactured by Stanley even more marketable. Wrought iron, the most common material for butts, was a rough substance with a pockmarked appearance. Hart thought he could boost sales by making the butts more attractive.

In his quest to improve the butt-manufacturing process, Hart convinced the other directors of The Stanley Works in 1869 to purchase the Philadelphia-based business of John Rankin, a company that was producing cast-iron butts ornamented with lead plates. Although the product was attractive, Rankin had little success selling the butts because the lead plates were soft.[2] Hart was intrigued, but he set aside the lead plate idea when, the following year, he obtained samples of lightweight hinges imported from Germany. "These hinges had a bright surface," Hart commented, "presumably produced by the use of emery wheels after hinges had been finished up to the point of polishing."[3]

"About the year 1870," Hart later told *Hardware Age*, "I suggested to Thomas Tracy, who

was in charge of the improvements at our butt factory, that he build a machine for polishing both sides of the iron plates from which we cut blanks for butts and hinges."[4] Tracy began the task, and also mentioned in passing that while manufacturing knitting machines, he had found a way to obtain a smooth surface on iron plates. The secret was to press cold plates through a set of rollers under high pressure, creating a uniform thickness and smooth surface.[5]

Soft metals such as copper, brass, silver and pewter had been cold-rolled for years, but the process produced material too brittle for use as hinges.[6]

Hart insisted on investigating this promising technique, and in 1870 he purchased a fine grade of Swedish iron plate and attempted to cold-roll it at the Bristol Brass Company's Rolling Mill.[7]

As a result of that experiment, in 1871 Hart bought a copper rolling mill in Boston, with the purpose of setting up a cold-rolling mill.[8] But the other directors of The Stanley Works would not allow him to build a place to house the machinery. "Our directors were so very conservative and strongly preju-

---

Above: A cast hinge, featured in the 1887 catalog of The Stanley Works.

diced against the words 'rolling mill' that we did not erect a building in which to install this set of rolls until 1873," Hart explained.[9] Until the structure was built, Hart and his assistants carted the iron six miles each way to a nearby town for cold-rolling at a brass rolling mill.[10] Purchasing the machine was a gamble that paid off handsomely, Hart noted.

"With my own hands, I operated that machinery and cold-rolled the Swedish iron, which started that day to revolutionize our business. We kept the secret for several years before competitors even dreamed of it, and in that period the Stanley Works became firmly entrenched financially."[11]

The iron emerged from the mill with a perfect finish and a uniform thickness. Since the hinges and the pin-guides formed by subsequent opera-

William Hart developed the telescope, or double, box in 1869 after he saw that merchants were wasting time looking for hinges and screws. The double box, which put the hinges and screws in the same package, was promoted by The Stanley Works well into the 20th century, as this promotional booklet (left) from about 1918 indicates. In addition to the boxes, The Stanley Works provided attractive display cases (opposite page) that showcased and organized Stanley products.

1869 – The Stanley Works purchases the John Rankin Company, manufacturer of cast-iron butts.

1871 – Hart purchases a copper rolling mill and establishes a cold-rolling mill.

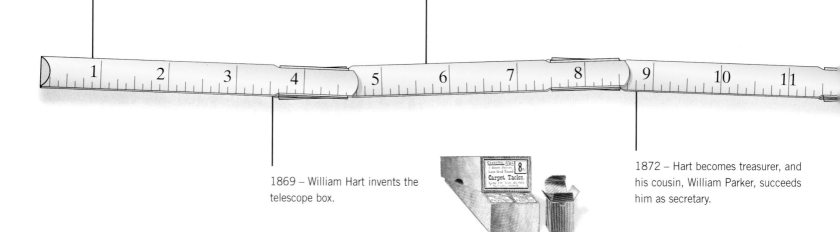

1869 – William Hart invents the telescope box.

1872 – Hart becomes treasurer, and his cousin, William Parker, succeeds him as secretary.

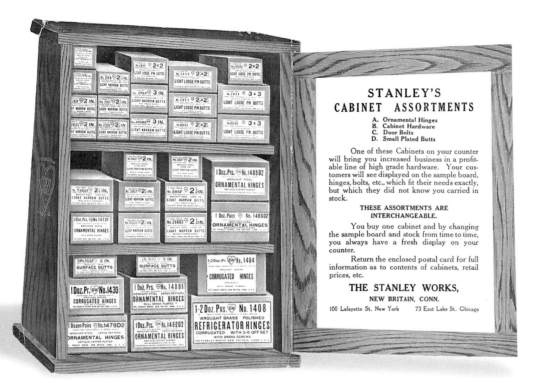

An Improved Form of Packaging

Hart was so involved in the day-to-day operations of The Stanley Works that he personally drove from store to store, collecting money, selling hardware and chatting with the merchants. Hart's granddaughter, Lillian Hart Tryon, wrote about these travels in a biographical sketch of her grandfather.

"Family and friends shared in the pleasure, which was no less keen because it was united with business. He directed the drives to country hardware and general stores, and counted the proprietors among his friends. They had a joke ready for his eager attention, and took him to inspect their shelves, and even into the cellars to look at the reserve stock. For years he himself took their orders for Stanley Works goods — a persuasive

tions were exactly the same size, the pins could be driven automatically using machines created by Tracy and others. This further benefit made the manufacturing process even more efficient, and consequently more profitable.[12]

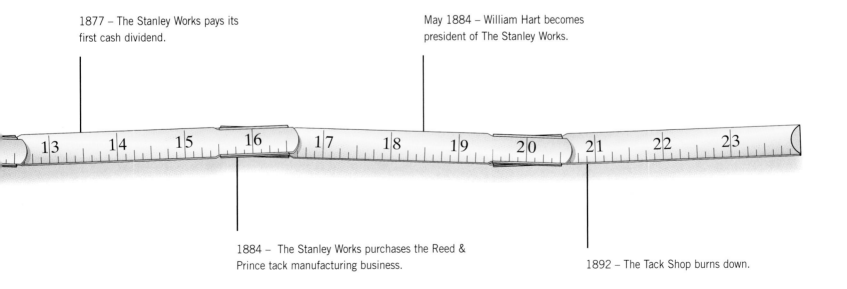

1877 – The Stanley Works pays its first cash dividend.

May 1884 – William Hart becomes president of The Stanley Works.

1884 – The Stanley Works purchases the Reed & Prince tack manufacturing business.

1892 – The Tack Shop burns down.

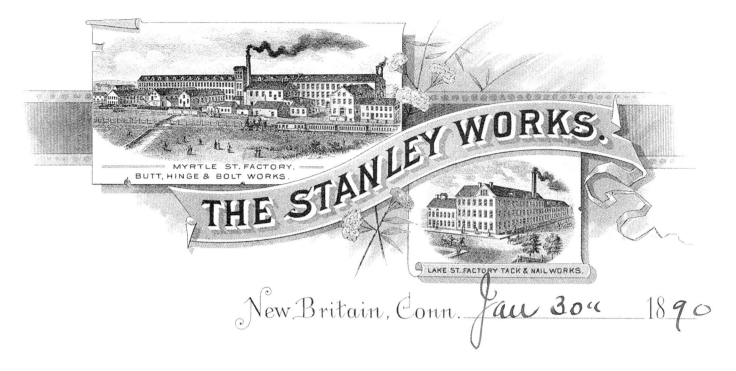

THE STANLEY WORKS.

MYRTLE ST. FACTORY.
BUTT, HINGE & BOLT WORKS.

LAKE ST. FACTORY TACK & NAIL WORKS.

New Britain, Conn. *Jan 30th* 1890

The Stanley Works' letterhead in the late 19th century.

salesman because of his sublime confidence in the superior quality of his wares.[13]

No detail escaped Hart's scrutiny when he visited the retail establishments. One of the many things that caught his attention was the way the proprietors stocked and packaged their merchandise, as Tryon described.

"Behind counters, peering into store rooms, and descending into basements, he was alert to catch all the circumstances of shelving, ticketing, spacing. In dim closets and cellars, 'often,' as he says, 'lighted only by candle or lantern,' he found the stock in paper packages, tied with strings and stuffed untidily into pigeon-holes, the labels as often as not being folded partly into the package, so that they could only be read by the man who put them up."[14]

Hart quickly realized that the existing system of packaging hinges separately from the screws required to mount them, made it difficult for merchants to match the two items. Hart saw this as inefficient and

began to work on a new style of packaging.

"As I wanted to print the class number and size of goods on labels in very large type which could be read from the floor when stored on upper shelves, and as I had decided to pack the goods in paper boxes, it was necessary to consider the shape of the boxes. This led me to make a telescope box, the first of its kind. I am sure that no

Above: Loose-joint butt hinges made in 1874 with Stanley cold-rolled iron. The hinge on the opposite page features a reversible acorn pin.

boxes of this description were ever made previous to this date. I believe this invention has been worth half a million dollars to The Stanley Works. James Roy, senior partner of Roy & Company, would not allow his general manager, Peter Roy, to change the packaging of wrought butts from the fine glazed-paper package to paper boxes until we had secured the preference throughout the entire country. He waited too long before adoption of this system, as when he did adopt this plan we had secured a large part of the business, which he was never able to regain."[15]

To convince dealers that selling hinges and screws separately was bad for business, Hart would occasionally go into a store where no one knew him and order a pair of 6-inch heavy strap hinges and the screws that were needed. As the clerk struggled to match the hinges with the requested screws,

The Stanley Works won this Certificate of Award for the line of cold-rolled hinges, butts and bolts it introduced at the International Exhibition in Philadelphia.

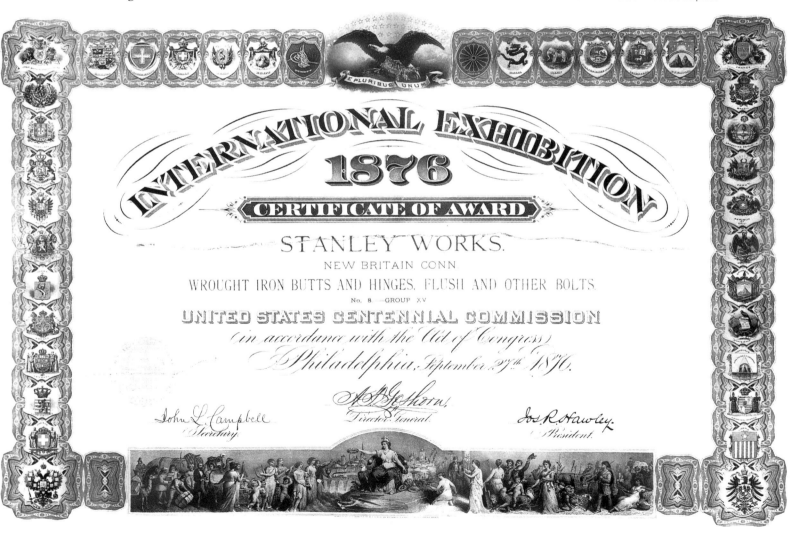

Hart would secretly time the proceedings with a stop watch carefully hidden in his pocket. He distributed his findings throughout the hardware industry, convincing both merchandisers and retailers that hinges and screws should be packaged together.[16]

"I didn't patent the idea," Hart later told a reporter. "It has never been patented; but I made the first double box. I made it, in the first place, because we needed it in our business, but I did not patent it and have never collected a penny in royalties from it. It was too useful a thing to the merchants of the world to be retarded by patents."[17]

By 1871, within two years of the introduction of the double box, The Stanley Works controlled half of the butt business in America.[18]

In 1872, Hart moved from the post of secretary and treasurer to that of treasurer, and his cousin, William Parker, succeeded him as secretary.[19] That year, with revenue reaching $480,000, Hart sought more

space, prompting stockholders to authorize an increase in capitalization to $260,000. The following year capitalization was increased to $300,000, and the company opened a New York sales office and began construction on a new building on the Myrtle Street property.[20]

Surviving a Financial Panic

Under the energetic guidance of William Hart, The Stanley Works continued to grow larger and more successful. But this exhilarating progress was slowed in 1873 by a worldwide financial panic that would hinder business throughout the nation for the next five years.[21] By the end of 1873, sales had diminished to such a degree that The Stanley Works discontinued work on its new building.

The company didn't have enough money to meet payroll, but Hart, unwilling to sacrifice valued employees, borrowed money to pay Stanley workers. He borrowed the maximum that local banks would allow, and when that money ran out, he began taking out personal loans.[22] Hart did not have trouble procuring the loans because he was a well-known and well-respected citizen of New Britain, serving as a director of the New Britain National Bank, a city councilman, and clerk and treasurer of the South Church of New Britain.[23]

Even when sales were dismal, Hart kept the factory running and the employees on the payroll. He simply stockpiled the merchandise they produced as inventory to be sold when the economy recovered. But when the other directors discovered Hart's borrowing habits, they demanded

A group of employees of The Stanley Works, 1885.

A rendering of New Britain in 1875.

an immediate curtailment of all production, as well as across-the-board reductions in salaries and wages, including those of the officers.

The directors did, however, recognize that the new cold-rolled hinges might be the solution to the company's economic troubles.[24] In 1875, they voted to produce a full line of "Smooth Bright Iron Heavy Narrow and Reversible Butts in addition to our line of ... Common iron," plus a line of "*Light* Strap & T-hinges, for the proper protection of existing trade."[25] They authorized an exhibit at the Philadelphia Centennial Exposition, at which The Stanley Works

received a Certificate of Award for "Wrought Iron Butts and Hinges, Flush and Other Bolts," by the United States Centennial Commission.[26]

Despite the honor of winning an important award, 1876 proved to be Stanley's worst year yet. Sales fell to $245,000, producing a loss of $13,500, its first real loss in twenty years.[27] On New Year's Day, 1877, the directors ordered drastic reductions in staff and production.[28] Fortunately, the cutbacks were soon found to be unnecessary. Sales began an upward trend in 1877, reaching $251,000 by year's end. The Stanley Works showed a profit, due in part to the sale of Hart's stockpiled inventory and his "new bright iron." That year, the company paid a cash dividend of 2.5 percent, and it hasn't stopped paying a dividend since.[29] The company's formula for success was summed up that year in *Asher & Adam's Pictorial Album of American Industry.*

"The secret of this company's success is an open one. All who will may avail themselves of it, and all who do so will succeed. One word tells it all, and that one word is — Excellence."[30]

The financial downturn even offered some advantages to The Stanley Works. In 1878, a New York machinery manufacturer called Crooke & Company, devastated by the slowed economy, offered to sell to The Stanley Works. Hart traveled to New York to evaluate the machinery, and elected to purchase it all, along with all titles and patents of the company, for $30,000.[31]

A Leader in Everything but Name

In 1877, at the age of 75, Frederick Stanley, the president of The Stanley Works, went completely blind. Though Stanley would remain president until his death in 1883, Hart became, more than ever, the leader of the company in everything but name.

By 1878, Hart held more Stanley stock than any other shareholder, continually reinvesting his money into the company for new equipment and other improvements. In November 1879, the directors authorized Hart to purchase and install electricity to replace the gas that was used to light Stanley's factory. The Stanley Works was lit by electricity a full six years before New Britain itself had electric light.[32]

Hart shared his simple philosophy of business with *Hardware Age* in 1918. "Commence early in life to establish a business you can own and control all your life, and don't increase that business beyond your own control."[33] He followed his own advice, controlling every detail of The Stanley Works' operation. It was said that he was "such a stickler for quality control that he would examine finished hinges at random with a magnifying glass,"[34] and he even opened all incoming mail himself, slitting the envelopes carefully so he could use the back for scrap paper.

"On mornings when he planned to leave for New York by the early train, with-

Above: A japanned wrought-iron parliament butt from the 1870 Stanley Works catalog. A japanned surface has a hard, brilliant, black varnish over the metal. Most of the hinges, butts, bolts and other wrought-iron products manufactured by The Stanley Works were available plain, japanned or bronzed.

Right: The Stanley Works, as pictured in the company's 1879 catalog.

out going to the factory, he would stop at the post office, get the mail, open it and fling it as fast as he read it into a basket, held by an office boy sent to meet him for that purpose. Often enough, the reading wouldn't be finished by train time, and Hart would stride to the station, still opening and reading letters, while the boy with the basket followed. Mounting the rear platform of the last coach, he would continue reading mail, tossing the letters as he finished with them to the waiting boy with the basket. And when the train crew (who, after all, had a connection to make at Berlin) finally pulled out, Hart would keep right on reading — and throwing the letters from the receding train to the panting boy who often had to run a quarter-mile down the track to recover the last letter. Not infrequently the office boy would be one of Hart's own [six] sons — which, perhaps, is one reason why a couple of them grew up to be track stars at Yale."[35]

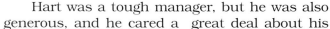

Hart was a tough manager, but he was also generous, and he cared a great deal about his employees. On one occasion, one of the young men at The Stanley Works had to travel due to poor health, and he didn't have enough money for his wife to accompany him. Hart sent the employee's wife a check to cover the expenses of the trip, saying that the employee would recover faster with his wife by his side.[36]

Industry Pools

During the 1870s and 1880s, manufacturers in several industries set up "pools," in which the members agreed to share the existing market, and in exchange, demanded that no member sell below the prices established by the pool. The pools discouraged newcomers, and even attempted to limit the sale of the machinery needed to manufacture the products.[37] Since modern antitrust laws did not yet exist, these pools were perfectly legal, and they were especially popular within the hardware trade.

The Stanley Works joined a hinge pool in the 1870s, but only because its competitors threatened to choke it out of the hinge business if it did not join. Hart didn't like the idea of joining the pool because doing so would benefit failing businesses such as Gilmore, Stanley's old competitor. Despite this aversion, The Stanley Works stayed in the pool for six years.

In 1882, Hart reluctantly joined The Tack Association pool, controlled by the Central Manufacturing Company of Boston. As part of the pool agreement, The Stanley Works used several

Above: A wrought-iron chest hinge (upper hinge) and a wrought-iron pew door hinge (lower hinge), from the company's 1870 price list. The chest hinge sold for $1.08 for one dozen pairs, and the pew door hinge was 84 cents per dozen pairs.

The Tack Shop and its employees, pictured in the 1880s.

machines controlled by the association, and hired skilled operators to run them.[38]

Then Hart learned of Reed & Prince, a Massachusetts company that manufactured tacks with its own custom-made machinery. By using its own machinery, Reed & Prince managed to operate independently of The Tack Association. Hart wanted to buy Reed & Prince, but his situation with the pool was delicate, so he had to proceed with caution.

"Hart appeared at Reed's office one morning, demanded, 'Do you want to sell your tack business?' — and declined to give his name or identify his connection. Reed — an equally canny

Yankee — declined to discuss business without knowing his visitor's name. So Hart walked out. A week or so later he repeated the performance — still with the same insistence on anonymity — and still with the same results. This time, however, he and Reed enjoyed each other's horse-trading company, and Hart on departing left with Reed a small wire-gauge he had in his pocket. It was one of a batch he'd had made up in the shop to his own design and he liked to give them to friends.

"Before he came back again, Reed had another visitor — a Canadian nail manufacturer named Britton, come to buy a tack machine. In the course of examining some of this equipment, Britton pulled out of his pocket a wire-gauge identical to Reed's. Said Reed, with seeming casualness, 'Where'd you get that?' 'Oh,' said the Canadian, 'that was given to me by the maker of

it — a good friend of mine in New Britain, Connecticut, named William H. Hart.' A week or two later, after Reed had spied the telltale wire-gauge, his mysterious visitor again stalked in, cloaked, he thought, in anonymity. Reed greeted him with, 'How do you do, Mr. William H. Hart of The Stanley Works?' Hart's chagrin disappeared, however, when Reed continued, 'Now, perhaps, we can talk business.' This put the final seal on Hart's liking for Reed. Now he wanted not only the machinery, patents and goodwill of the business, but Reed and his partner Prince as well, for The Stanley Works." [39]

Hart purchased the business for $25,000 worth of Stanley stock and brought the two founders, Reed and Prince, along with their wives, to New Britain. In March 1884, Hart hired the two men and set them up in the former Knob Furnace located across the street from The Bolt Manufactory. The building, which had been vacant since Hart moved The Stanley Works to Myrtle Street, was renamed The Tack Shop. [40]

The Tack Shop

When The Tack Shop began production, it was not particularly lucrative. Since all tacks are basically alike, it was difficult to make a superior or markedly different product. By the end of 1891, directors of The Stanley Works were losing enthusiasm for tacks, a feeling shared even by Reed and Prince, who busied themselves inventing machinery to manufacture wood screws, a venture for which The Stanley Works showed little enthusiasm. [41]

In June 1892, The Tack Shop burned down, the flames fueled by oil spattered on its wood frame from years of manufacture. [42] With the end of The Tack Shop came the end of Stanley's attempt at manufac-turing tacks, and from that day forward, the company never again ventured into the tack business.

The fire had its advantages, however. Hart managed to salvage the burned, fused-together tacks from the debris and separated them for sale in bulk. The Tack Shop's land, along with another plot of land across the street, was sold to Russell & Erwin for $12,500. Reed and Prince moved to Worcester, Massachusetts, and set up a business with the sole purpose of manufacturing wood screws, which eventually became one of the largest companies of its kind in the world. [43]

The Stanley Works refused to join any other pools, even though doing so might have been profitable.

In August 1883, Frederick T. Stanley passed away at the age of 81. He had been president of The Stanley Works from the day he founded it in 1843 until the day he died. In addition to his outstanding business record, Stanley was a leading citizen of his community, as his obituary in the local newspaper indicated.

"His accumulations would have been much greater except for his generosity in the giving of his means and time for the benefit of others, and especially the advancement of the public interests. ... New Britain by reason of his life is richer by far in all its substantial interests, business, social, educational, and religious." [44]

Frederick's distant cousin, Henry Stanley, who was a director of The Stanley Works, was elected to fill the vacant position of company president. Unfortunately, Henry himself passed away just a few months later, in May 1884. [45] William Hart filled the seat, adding the presidency to his title of treasurer of The Stanley Works, and "making him in name, as well as in fact, the head of the firm." [46]

The fictional Stanley Lady appeared in export catalogs in the 1890s and helped increase the company's growing international presence.

CHAPTER FOUR

BRANCHING OUT

"Mr. Hart has been granted 29 patents for improved machinery, and every one of them has been turned over to his company without charge."

— Historian Robert Leavitt[1]

IN 1890, THE Stanley Works employed 350 men and 150 women, and manufactured a broad line of merchandise, including "every variety of hinge, together with bolts, brackets and other staple items of builders' hardware."[2] The company was regarded as among the best employers in town. One employee told a reporter, "When it came time for me to look for a job [in the 1890s], my mother said, 'Try The Stanley Works first; I notice, watching out the window as the men and women pass, that they look like the kind of people I'd want my boy to work with — self-respecting folks that probably lay up an extra dollar when they earn it.'"[3]

Another employee reminisced about his 51 years of service at The Stanley Works in a 1938 article distributed to Stanley employees.

"In March 1874, while still a boy of 12, I entered the employ of the Stanley Plant. ... From my entrance to my retirement in December 1925, I valued and respected my employers for their integrity and attitude toward their employees, and I can say that I thoroughly enjoyed my long connection with the company."[4]

In the 1890s, each department was run by an independent contractor whose pay was based on the number of units produced. The contractors hired their own help, paying a set rate for each unit produced. To earn a profit, the contractor could either hire cheap workers and overwork them, or hire a higher quality of worker and improve his manufacturing process. By improving the process, both the contractor and the factory worker increased output and earned more money.[5]

Some employees regarded the contractor-run departments as more efficient than their foreman-run counterparts. One critic of the foreman system was E. Allen Moore, who started with The Stanley Works in 1889 as an office clerk, and whose specialty was evaluating costs. Moore, who would become president of The Stanley Works in 1918, was an artist's son who couldn't afford to attend college. Despite his lack of formal education, he demonstrated considerable knowledge of industrial operations, and in running a business.[6] He also had the "mixed advantage and disadvantage of marrying the boss's daughter," Martha Elizabeth Hart.[7]

Moore once wrote, "The contractor system did more for improved processes than those departments conducted by foremen on a salary basis. Foremen were paid a salary, had keys to a back gate, came and went when they felt like it, and were little interested in their costs."[8]

Above: T-hinge pictured in an insert for the 1894 Stanley Works catalog.

The Stanley Works factory and office building as it looked in 1895.

Stanley Works' executives kept a sharp eye on both contractors and foremen, and the result was that The Stanley Works was generally regarded as a good place to work, wrote historian Robert Leavitt.

"Old-timers who can remember those days, or who have heard of them from their fathers, tell how companionable it used to be in this or that department, with a well-liked foreman or contractor and a congenial group at the benches. ... Vendors of fruit, hot dogs or other refreshments used to come by on Myrtle Street, so that if a man on an upper floor lowered a pail with a nickel in it, he could draw up in return enough bananas or peaches for himself and his helper, with maybe a cent or two in change. And (it was said around town) at The Stanley Works you didn't have to

January 31, 1888 – Corrugated hinges are patented.

1899 – The Stanley Works purchases the Bridgewater Iron Company.

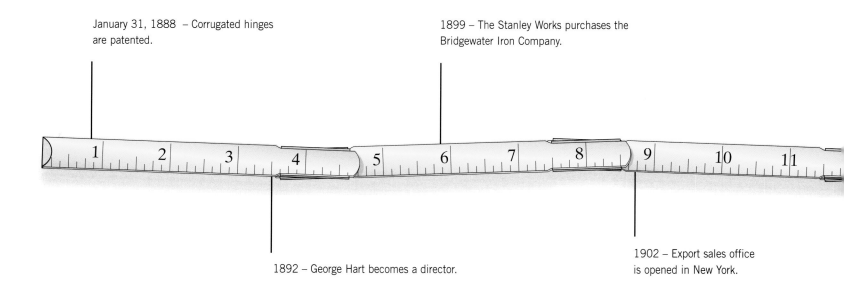

1892 – George Hart becomes a director.

1902 – Export sales office is opened in New York.

Right: A hinge featuring the corrugated design that was patented January 31, 1888 by William H. Hart and Thomas Corscaden. The strength and affordability of corrugated hinges made them popular with customers. (Walter Jacob photograph/Charles and Walter Jacob collection.)

Below: A paperweight from The Stanley Works, showing the patented corrugated steel hinge. (Walter Jacob photograph/Charles and Walter Jacob collection.)

watch that pail on the way up, to guard against it being intercepted by someone with an appetite but no nickel, on a lower floor.

"The few who didn't tote their lunches would stoke up at Halinan's Bakery Shop, on Myrtle Street, where doughnuts were 5¢ the half-dozen. From Halinan's, too, used to come the doughnuts and coffee which William H. Hart would order in for people working overtime." [9]

The Bridgeport Rolling Mill

In 1891, The Stanley Works increased its capitalization to $400,000, and pro-duced a record number of cold-rolled steel items. One of its steel suppliers was the nearby Bridgeport Rolling Mill, a facility so small that The Stanley Works was its largest customer. When the mill faced financial difficulties, Hart decided to lease the business, "not because he wanted to operate a steel business, but to protect his supply of a vital raw material." [10]

The lease was discontinued in 1893 when Connecticut suffered a sharp economic panic, followed by a brief recession. The Stanley Works was able to take advantage of the situation, buying steel from independent suppliers at a price below the cost of manufacture. [11] Without Stanley's business, the Bridgeport Mill had no customers and was forced to put itself up for sale. Hart could have purchased it, but he elected

1905 – The company builds a new boiler plant.

1907 – New office building is completed.

1906 – A nine-story building is constructed on the land purchased in 1871.

IN 1900, THE STANLEY WORKS published a small, whimsically illustrated pamphlet called *The Autobiography of S. Corrugated Hinge*. "I am known as The Stanley Corrugated Steel Hinge," the narrative began. "It is not everyone who can rightly put the word 'The' before his name. That title is used by kings and lords of a high degree; but I consider myself entitled to it by my pre-eminence among all kinds of hinges."

Written in the first person, the pamphlet noted that The Stanley Corrugated Steel Hinge, patented January 31, 1888, featured corrugations, or folds, that surrounded the pin and extended along the hinge, adding tremendous strength without increasing the price of the hinge.

The Autobiography of S. Corrugated Hinge

"For years, my owners had been making my ancestors, the old style Strap and T-Hinges, and had been trying to devise something that should be an improvement on them. I can point with pride to one of my predecessors, to which even today I must acknowledge myself inferior. I refer to what is known as Hart's Patent Strap and T-Hinges. ...

Two thicknesses of iron surrounded the pin throughout its length and extend upon the straps of the Hinge, thus giving double thickness of iron at the points where most needed, and more than double the strength of an ordinary strap hinge.

"But the cost of these Hart's Patent Hinges is necessarily considerably higher than the ordinary kind, so that their use is limited to places where the best is wanted without regard to price. You will find them used on refrigerator car doors, etc. But one source of my great popularity is, that while I am infinitely better and stronger than the old style hinges, I am sold at the same price.

"I am somewhat lighter than the old style, which enables me to save you unnecessary expense in freight (and duties, if you live in a foreign country), and makes me easier to handle. And last but not least, by improved methods of manufacture and the purchase of costly machinery, my makers are able to put me on the market at a price which is practically the same as that of the ordinary hinge."[12]

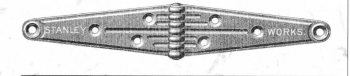

Above and left: Illustrations from *The Autobiography of S. Corrugated Hinge.*

not to, remaining faithful to his basic philosophy of business, which forbade "increasing the business beyond his own control."[13]

Hart simply wasn't good at delegating authority. Almost everything that happened at The Stanley Works was directed across his desk for final approval. It was during this period that Thomas Corscaden, an inventor who had recently come to The Stanley Works, said to Moore, "He is too busy with the business to do business."[14] Hart was so busy that he didn't give a thought to the condition of his office. E.A. Moore described what a visitor would encounter upon entering the room.

"Here was The Stanley Works' office, about forty feet square. High bookkeeper's desks, a press to copy all letters and one typewriter for the single stenographer, or 'typewriter,' as she was generally called. Two small private offices, one for the president and the other used by his assistant and cost clerk, where the single telephone and the watchman's time clock hung on the wall. The washbowl — cold water only — was in the adjoining packing room. The one closet [toilet] was off the Main Office stair-landing between floors. One small immovable pane of glass with an interior outlook lighted the place enough to read. I remember I lost a five-dollar bill somewhere about the office and posted a notice. Two weeks afterward Eddie Irving found it on the floor of the dingy room where it had rested undiscovered by eye or broom for a fortnight."[15]

William Hart continually sought new ways to improve the company. Pleased with Stanley's success in cold-rolling iron, he wondered if other metals would respond to the same procedure. He was especially interested in cold-rolling steel and, between 1880 and 1890, he worked tirelessly toward this goal. After 10 frustrating years, his dedication paid off, as he described to a reporter in 1918.

"I finally found a steel sufficiently ductile for rolling into strips. This process we also kept a secret. In fact, the process was ours exclusively for six years before things got out, and during that period we were a thorn in the flesh of com-

Cold-Rolled Wrought Steel

THE STANLEY WORKS was the first company to cold-roll steel for butts, hinges, bolts and brackets. The process produced steel that was stronger, more durable and more attractive than steel produced by the previous method of hot-rolling. The beautiful cold-rolled items shown here were featured in a 1901 pamphlet prepared for the Pan-American Exposition in Buffalo, New York.

Above: A wrought-steel door bolt.

Center: A corrugated wrought-steel and brass ornamental hinge.

Right: A wrought-steel loose pin butt, with a raised surface in light bronze.

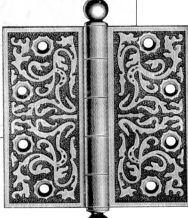

petitors. They couldn't understand our costs, nor did they approach the brightness of our goods. The manufacture of cold-rolled steel overcame some of the most difficult problems in the butt and hinge business."[16]

William Hart's son, George Hart, became president of The Stanley Works in 1915, and served as chairman from 1918 to 1923.

With his invention of a method to cold-roll steel butts and hinges, Hart added to an already impressive list of firsts for The Stanley Works.

"The Stanley Works made the first hinge hasp; the first crate hinge; the first corrugated hinge; the first hinge with a reinforced joint; the first New York City blind hinge of solid metal; the first barrel bolt, where the barrel was made of one piece; the first neck bolt; the first wrought-iron center bolt; the first wrought butts; the first wrought butts with loose pins (they were reversible, and sounded the death knell of right and left butts and greatly reduced the stocks necessarily carried by jobbers and retailers); the first wrought butts of cold-rolled iron, and then cold-rolled steel; and the

first corrugated butts. His factory was the first to drive butt and hinge pins by machinery, and the first to rivet pins by machinery. Mr. Hart has been granted 29 patents for improved machinery, and every one of them has been turned over to his company without charge." [17]

George Hart and E.A. Moore

When William Hart's son, George, graduated from high school, he was hired as a salesman by The Stanley Works, becoming a director in 1892.[18] George Hart was an able and popular negotiator, and his territory was Stanley's most profitable. He was loved throughout the company, "not as Hart's son but for his singularly magnetic personality and fine character." [19]

Although George Hart was the son of the president, and E.A. Moore was married to the daughter of the president, neither man could expect preferential treatment from William Hart. If anything, Hart demanded more from these two men than he did from other employees. Since George Hart was a salesman, his contribution to the company could be evaluated by his sales record. Moore's work, however, fell more directly under Hart's watchful eye, and the different business styles of the two men sometimes led to conflict, as Leavitt noted.

"[Moore's] views were modern where Hart's were outdated; his methods coldly and accurately impersonal where Hart's were warmly if sometimes erratically human. If Hart had been a weaker man, he would have repressed rather than encouraged Moore. It is to his credit, therefore, that while he would not make Moore an officer until 1905, he did allow him from the start to accomplish an increasing number of changes in the business." [20]

Moore could boast of many accomplishments during his years moving up the ranks at Stanley. He initiated new record-keeping procedures that could differentiate between profitable and unprofitable products, devised an inventory system, oversaw the remodeling of old buildings and the construction of new ones, set up machinery that allowed the company to produce its own boxes, and established a department to design and build machines. He also hastened the elimination of the contractor system, replacing it with a program that allowed employees to work on an equal basis.[21]

At the end of the 19th century, it was common for competitors to join together, creating a large corporation known as a trust. Stanley's steel suppliers created such a conglomerate, a move that promptly raised steel prices for customers such as The Stanley Works. Hart realized that his company could prosper only if it could produce its own iron and steel, thereby controlling its availability.

By then, the Bridgeport Rolling Mill that had been on the market in 1891 was no longer available. In 1899, The Stanley Works purchased The Bridgewater Iron Company in Bridgewater, Massachusetts. The plant would be used to hot-roll steel, which would later be shipped to New Britain for cold-rolling.

Stanley paid $45,000 for the company, less than the cost of building a new plant, but still a handsome sum, given that in 1894 Hart himself earned only $6,000 per year.[22] But Hart figured that the mill was worth $40,000 a year in reduced steel costs and prompt service to customers alone.[23]

Stepping Aside for a New Generation

With the addition of the Bridgewater Iron Company, Stanley became "an integrated industry, producing its own raw material. As the old century passed into the new, The Stanley Works passed from a large Manufactory into a small Big Business."[24] With the new expansion, Hart finally relaxed his control over the company. He took a few years off to recuperate from nervous prostration and hardening of the arteries.[25]

George Hart and E.A. Moore ran the business during William Hart's absence, and, in general, the two were pleased to have the older man out of the picture. As Moore later wrote, "We were each carrying our responsibilities most successfully, and were free to develop the business without considering anyone's opinion but our own, subject, of course, to the

approval of the directors. We consulted and worked together with great confidence in each other."[26]

The Sales Department

Before George Hart took control of The Stanley Works' sales, there had been a complete lack of organization related to the sale of Stanley products. Hart divided the department into three areas of responsibility. Peter McCartee, a vice president, controlled sales in New York and the southern states, and was responsible for the company's small but growing export business. George Hart directed sales for all states from the Midwest to the Pacific Ocean. All other sales responsibilities were handled by L. Hoyt Pease.

George Hart established the first sales department in the history of The Stanley Works, gradually

Ethelbert Allen Moore started working for The Stanley Works in 1889. He served as president of the company from 1918 to 1923 and chairman from 1923 to 1929.

increasing the number of wholesale distributors across the country. He sent his younger brother, Edward Hart, to South Africa with a full line of Stanley products to distribute. In 1902, George Hart opened an export sales office in New York under Edward's management, and built a substantial business in Europe, Latin America and the Pacific area, including Australia and New Zealand.[27]

As The Stanley Works grew, the company became a sought-after resource for manufacturers seeking specialty hinges of unusual sizes or designs. These orders were expensive for the company to handle because normal operations had to be interrupted to produce relatively small quantities of the special-request items.[28]

By 1905, The Stanley Works was dealing with such a high volume of these specialty orders that Moore started a separate department to handle them, and George Hart established a sales force exclusively for these custom designs. The Stanley Works soon boasted between $5,000 and $6,000 a month in special-order business.[29]

The improved sales organization boosted Stanley's revenues, and it contributed to George Hart's enormous personal popularity in the hardware business, "a popularity enhanced by such gestures as his shipping carload after carload of goods into fire-stricken San Francisco after its 1906 disaster." Hart reportedly said, "Never mind when they can pay. They need the stuff."[30]

Expansion and Modernization

The market for hardware continued to expand as the nation grew, and new kinds of hinges came into demand. To meet the increased requirements, The Stanley Works expanded and updated its facilities. By 1901, Stanley was using electric locomotives in its yards, followed shortly thereafter by electric crane equipment and, eventually, by magnetic cranes for handling material and scrap.[31] Four years later, in 1905, the company built a new boiler plant across the tracks from the engine room. The plant was the first in New Britain to use automatic stok-

A steam-powered yard engine, used only for short hauling between buildings. The engine, which had no firebox or boiler, was charged with steam each day. It is now on display at the Trolley Museum in Warehouse Point, Connecticut.

ing, a process that substantially reduced the amount of smoke that was released.[32] In 1906, a nine-story building for storage and shipment was erected on the triangle of land that Hart had purchased in 1871. It was the largest concrete building in New Britain.[33]

That same year, the directors authorized Moore to spend $50,000 constructing a new office building that would connect to the factory buildings by way of two bridges over the intervening railroad tracks. Moore and an architect spent several months designing the building, and then sought bids. The lowest was higher than $80,000. The plan was revised, but the lowest bid this time around was still more than $60,000. The architect told Moore that it would be impossible to finish the building for less, but Moore refused to ask the directors for more money, insisting it could be accomplished for under $50,000. Five months after Moore started collecting bids, he phoned a well-known Boston architect named Bertram Taylor, and invited him to Hartford. Moore later described the meeting.

In 1907, The Stanley Works moved into new corporate offices on Lake Street in New Britain. The beautiful Italian Renaissance-style building was designed by renowned architect Bertram Taylor.

"After talking things over we took a private room in the Hartford Club about three in the afternoon and when we finished at about 2 a.m. the next morning, the preliminary plans for the main office building were complete and had nothing in common with the plans made by the other architect. Very shortly the specifications and drawings were submitted to contractors, resulting in a low bid of $44,000 by one of the best builders in the state — the H. Wales Lines Company of Meriden. The contract was signed October 16, 1906, and we moved into the building with its new furniture (flat-top mahogany desks instead of the old roll-tops) and general overhead lighting system, designed by the General Electric Company, on October 1, 1907, considering ourselves very up-to-date in our new quarters." [34]

The building was styled after the Italian Renaissance period, with the interior inspired by the Bank of France in Paris. Moore didn't want employees to socialize with business visitors, so he included private offices only for the top executives and provided several consulting rooms for everybody else to use.

WHETHER you are planning to build a new garage or are just dissatisfied with the fit tings on your present one, you will be mighty interested in seeing samples of the shipment of *Stanley Garage Hardware* we have just received and which we are displaying this week in our window.

is so different from the usual hardware you might have put on your garage that we won't even try to tell you here, any more about it. You will understand as soon as you see our display.

Garage owners, who have equipped their garages with this hardware, tell us how satisfactorily it works, and how greatly it adds to the service they get from having their own garages.

We have a line of gasoline pumps, garage heaters, automobile tubes, vulcanizers, etc. In fact, you can get here, whatever you may require for your automobile or your garage.

A. BAUER & CO.
BALTIMORE, MD.

C1

A 1917 advertisement for Stanley garage hardware, introduced by The Stanley Works in 1914.

CHAPTER FIVE

A NEW CENTURY BRINGS A NEW GENERATION

"I prefer to receive less credit myself and award full credit to all associated with me during the past twenty-five years who have rendered such excellent service in developing the business and who have contributed so largely to the success of this company."

— William Hart, 1915[1]

THOUGH WILLIAM HART returned to The Stanley Works in 1902, he never completely regained the power he had held in earlier years. A new generation had taken the helm of the company, as E.A. Moore explained.

"When Mr. Hart Senior partially recovered, he came back into the business still the president. I was almost 40 and he was over 70. It is easy to imagine how hard it was for him to see things going along better than ever, not knowing the reason for many changes, feeling not very strong and rather out of it because of his long absence. His friends tried to have him remain as president, but give up much of the active management."[2]

Hart did lessen his control, and resigned as treasurer in 1904.[3] The post was filled by L. Hoyt Pease, hired by Hart some 40 years earlier. Pease's son, Maurice Pease, and his grandson, Hoyt Curtis Pease, also worked for The Stanley Works. "Between the three of us, there were 74 or 75 years of service on the board of directors," said Hoyt Curtis Pease in a recent interview. "My uncle, Maurice, was on the board for quite a while. He ran the Steel Division for a good many years."[4]

Hart, still president, continued to be very active in the community. He was a director of two local banks, the YMCA, and the New Britain General Hospital, and had served as an officer of the city of New Britain, the South Church of New Britain, and the New Britain Club. Everyone in town knew him for his energy and liveliness, as well as for the important positions he held. "He had an electric automobile — an open runabout — in which he persisted in driving around New Britain, even after his eyesight had begun to fail, at a rate that caused wise people to jump hastily for the sidewalks."[5]

Increased Efficiency

In supplying the Midwest and West with heavy hinges, The Stanley Works had been paying heavy freight charges to and from New Britain. In 1907, the company purchased 30 acres of land in Niles, Ohio, to establish a regional factory to reduce high shipping charges. The land was located near the

---

Above: This rendering is a 1908 Stanley Works booklet promoting ball-bearing hinges. The booklet notes that several New York landmarks, including the Hotel Astor and the United States Express Company Building, were equipped with the hinges.

Mahoning River and the Pennsylvania, Baltimore and Ohio and Erie Railroads, making it a convenient shipping site.[6]

The plant was equipped with the latest in modern technology, and by 1911, employees at the Niles plant were using conveyor-line production methods that hadn't been tried yet, even in the automobile industry.[7]

Meanwhile, the Bridgewater Iron Company plant was remodeled, expanding its capacity to 46,000 tons of hot-rolled strip steel per year.[8] The iron company was so efficient that it was able to produce a hefty surplus of steel that The Stanley Works could sell to other industrial concerns. By 1911, The Stanley Works was selling more than $1 million worth of excess steel a year.[9]

As the company continued to purchase land and build new properties, William Hart remained adamantly in the thick of every deal. He loved to negotiate, and he generally prevailed, as he noted with pride in a 1919 letter to his son, Walter.

"In making all of these purchases of property, I have never been blackmailed except in the pur-

An advertisement for Stanley garage hardware from approximately 1920.

1907 — The Stanley Works purchases 30 acres of land in Niles, Ohio.

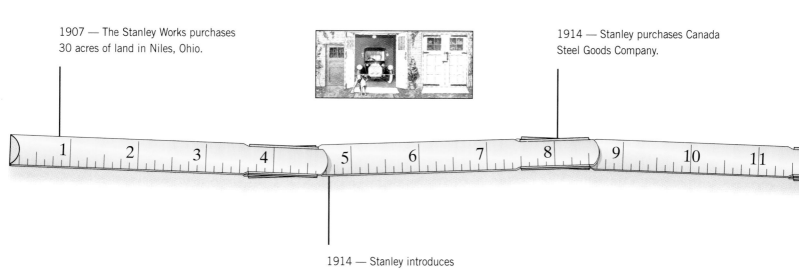

1914 — Stanley purchases Canada Steel Goods Company.

1914 — Stanley introduces garage door hardware sets.

chase of the land of the Sovereign Trading Company, where one of the directors apparently held a position equivalent to that of Kaiser Wilhelm, but I have never regretted the purchase of that property."[10]

The Stanley Chemical Company

E.A. Moore's quest to improve the quality of cold-rolled steel production prompted him, in 1909, to hire chemist William Rowland. Working with Moore, Rowland made several important contributions to the cold-rolling process, making it possible to reclaim and recycle the valuable sulphite and iron, as well as eliminate wastes such as acid that were harmful to sewage beds. But, as Moore later explained, Rowland soon found half of his time idle, "as a company of our size did not seem to have chemical problems enough to keep him occupied."[11]

In an effort to keep busy, Rowland decided to tackle the problem of reclaiming waste metals that could not be used because they were mixed with dirt and ashes. Moore felt that the pursuit of this goal would be a worthwhile venture, as he later explained.

"I agreed to personally finance a partnership, [Rowland] to work half-time for The Stanley Works and half for the new project. Later we

incorporated the enterprise under the General Statutes of the State under the modest name of the Connecticut Metal and Chemical Company with authorized capital of $50,000, of which $2,500 was paid in. The papers were signed September 9, 1911, and approved the following day. At first we rented a small factory with a little water power and plenty of water near Bristol, and after several months' work had learned much about the reclamation of metal wastes in Connecticut, lost some money, but saw our way clear to pursue the business successfully."[12]

When Moore informed company directors that he was working on this new project, they in turn reminded him that his salary was for employment with The Stanley Works.[13] They decided to consolidate the ventures, and in 1916 The Stanley Works purchased the chemical company and moved it to New Britain. In 1921, the enterprise was renamed the Stanley Chemical Company.

Moore also found a way to shape cold-rolled steel into a "cup" shape for products requiring a bulging or hollowed piece of metal. The technique became extremely popular for production of such items as movie theater candy machines. Out of that activity grew Stanley's Pressed Metal Division, one of the company's busiest departments.

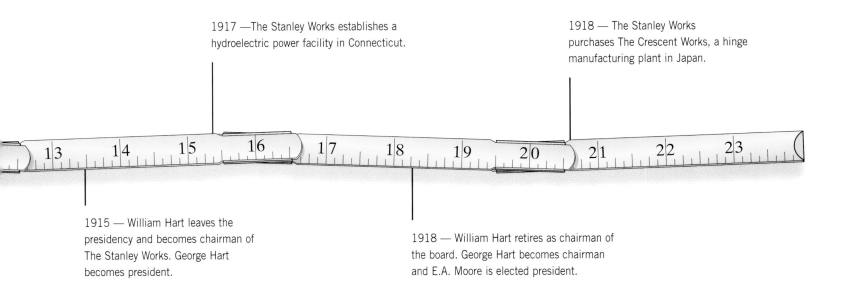

1917 —The Stanley Works establishes a hydroelectric power facility in Connecticut.

1918 — The Stanley Works purchases The Crescent Works, a hinge manufacturing plant in Japan.

1915 — William Hart leaves the presidency and becomes chairman of The Stanley Works. George Hart becomes president.

1918 — William Hart retires as chairman of the board. George Hart becomes chairman and E.A. Moore is elected president.

When you build your garage, be sure to have swinging doors

*T*HIS *type of construction permits all entrances to be opened at the same time.*

has been especially designed for garage use. Doors hung on Stanley Hinges close weather tight—and Stanley fastenings keep them so.

Swinging doors equipped with Stanley Hinges take no inside space and open and close easily and smoothly, without sagging or sticking.

Write to-day for booklet P-5 on Stanley Garage Hardware. It will be of interest to you. All the better Hardware Dealers carry Stanley Garage Hardware in stock or will gladly get it for you.

THE STANLEY WORKS
New Britain, Conn., U. S. A.

New York: Chicago:
100 Lafayette St.   73 East Lake St.

Meanwhile, The Stanley Works continued to introduce new products and divisions. By 1914, the automobile had become an established part of American life, and many homes were being built with garages. That year, Stanley introduced garage door hardware sets, which included all necessary parts and screws for installation.[14]

A Policy of Acquisition

Around 1915, The Stanley Works adopted a strategic policy of acquiring other companies.[15] The Stanley Works had been interested in building a plant in Canada, eager to tap into a market that was increasing with the population. In 1914, the company purchased the Canada Steel Goods Company of Hamilton, Ontario, makers of builder's hardware.[16] Buying the concern meant that The Stanley Works could enter the Canadian market with an established, well-run factory and competent management. The Canadian plant proved so successful that within a short period of time, it added pressed metal products to its hardware line.[17] In 1916, a cold-rolling operation, the Stanley Steel Company, Ltd., was built next door to the Canadian facility. For many years, it was the only plant in Canada capable of producing cold-rolled steel.[18]

The Stanley Works had two more opportunities to purchase the Bridgeport Rolling Mill that had been on the market in 1894 and which it wanted to purchase in 1899. In both 1911 and 1913, the Bridgeport Mill, by then known as The American Tube and Stamping Company, was offered to Stanley. Automobiles were becoming important customers for steel, and The Stanley Works might have profited considerably by selling steel to the auto industry. E.A. Moore was enthusiastic about the possibility, but William Hart and the directors didn't want to expand the steel operation beyond what had already been established. When The Stanley Works declined to purchase the mill in 1911, two members of the Tube and Stamping Company's board of directors tried to persuade Moore to leave Stanley and take control of the stamping company.[19] Moore considered the offer, rationalizing that, "The Stanley

A 1918 advertisement for Stanley garage hardware.

Works would be better off to have me as a competitor in cold-rolled steel than any stranger operating the Bridgeport business."[20] But Moore eventually elected to remain where he was and continue his rise in responsibility at The Stanley Works.

William Hart Becomes Chairman

In 1915, following a remarkable 61 years of service to the company, William Hart retired from the presidency of The Stanley Works and began serving as chairman of the board. In his honor, the company established the sweetheart logo that rapidly became a symbol of Stanley quality. Hart's son, George Hart, took over as president. Shortly after the transition, William Hart reminisced with a reporter from *Hardware Age* magazine.

"Referring to my sixty years' service as an officer of this company, I feel under great obligations to the several boards of directors who have elected me and given me their counsel and support for so many years. For a period of about thirty years of the first thirty-five years, owing to the ill health of both Frederick and William Stanley and the blindness of Frederick Stanley, the responsibility of the business rested mainly on my shoulders and I am willing to accept a reasonable portion of the credit that has been shown in appreciation of such services."

"During the past twenty-five years there has been a steady growth and as the business has increased my associates have willingly assumed additional responsibilities to match and more than match the growth of the business. I prefer not to mention names of the efficient men who have rendered valuable service, as if I once began I would not know where to stop. I prefer to receive less credit myself and award full credit to all associated with me during the past twenty-five years who have rendered such excellent service in developing the business and who have contributed so largely to the success of this company." [21]

William H. Hart was president of The Stanley Works from 1884 to 1915, and chairman from 1915 to 1918. He served as a director until his death the following year.

It was a typical gesture from the leader of a remarkable company. Executives at The Stanley Works have always credited employees with the success of the company, and have worked hard to create a rewarding work environment. In addition to providing excellent employment opportunities, The Stanley Works took such measures as providing English classes to the European immigrants who were living in New Britain and working at The Stanley Works.

New Sources of Power

Since the early 1900s, The Stanley Works had been using hydroelectric power at the Bridgewater Iron Company in Massachusetts, and the arrangement

William and Martha Hart touring New Britain in their car.

war, the operation was discontinued and Bridge-water again became Stanley's main source of steel for cold-rolling.

Four hundred and fifty men and women from The Stanley Works served in World War I, and 13 gave their lives.[26] During the war, The Stanley Works established a newsletter called *The Stanley Workers*, which helped Stanley employees keep in touch with their friends serving overseas. The newsletters were sent to soldiers, along with gifts such as tobacco, chocolate and mirrors. The newsletter frequently published letters from soldiers, such as this March 1918 letter from Ross Rhodes, Machine Gun Company, 102nd Inf. A.E.F.

"You can't imagine our feeling on receiving those little gifts, and that paper. Gee, it seems darn good to get some first hand news from Old U.S.A. I received my first copy today and read through it several times. You no doubt know from letters which you have received that it is darned lonesome over here. We have lots of lonely days and exciting days, but no pleasures to speak of."[27]

Edson S. Smith, Lt. Sig. R.C.A.S., wrote in January 1918.

"I received The Stanley Workers and the trench mirror last week and was more than glad to receive them. A person loses his identity so completely in a large camp that any remembrance from home is greatly appreciated. ... I notice Stanley Works' hinges at every turn, and find great satisfaction in pointing out that I am from the town where they are made."[28]

The Stanley Workers proved so popular that the company continued to publish it after the war ended. Eventually renamed *The Stanley World*, the newsletter was written by and for employees. It clearly demonstrated the feelings of pride and friendship shared by Stanley Works' employees.

William Hart's Departure

In January 1918, William Hart retired as chairman of the board at the age of 84. He told *Hardware Age*, "I have resigned my position ... it feels like I can now indulge in reminiscences."[29] Journalist Roy F. Soule included his own impressions of Hart's 63 years with The Stanley Works.

"Mr. Hart is now an old man, but his memory for dates, places, men and occurrences is truly marvelous. He gives you the impression of a man who loves the whole world, and his affection is returned in full measure by the hardware men of America. ... To come in contact with the grand old man of New Britain is to recharge the cells of faith in yourself and in your fellow man."[30]

Upon Hart's resignation, George Hart became the chairman of the board, Moore became president, and Clarence F. Bennett was elected vice president

in charge of New Britain and Niles, Ohio, operations. Bennett had joined the company in 1891 as a shipping room hand.

From left to right: Stanley truck drivers A. Guadette, H. Spencer, J. Horlock and C. Karie stand beside their vehicles in 1919.

"The story goes that he had caught William Hart's eye while sweeping the sidewalk in front of the plumbing supply store where he worked — a task he disliked and accordingly did fast and furiously to get it over with. Hart, passing by, stopped and asked, 'Do you always sweep as hard as this?' 'Yes, sir,' said the boy. 'Come and work the same way for me,' said Hart, 'and I'll see that you don't regret it.' And he was as good as his word." [31]

In February 1918, George Hart purchased controlling interest in a small Japanese hinge manufacturing plant, based in Kobe, called The Crescent Works. The Stanley Works moved the company to Osaka, where it continued making hardware for the Far Eastern market until 1926, when signs of Japanese imperialism became clear and Stanley sold the plant.[32]

William Hart passed away on December 13, 1919, at the age of 85. His obituary began, "No town has produced a better man than William Hart of New Britain who died yesterday morning." [33]

He had been a director of The Stanley Works from 1856 until his death. During his lifetime, he watched a $30,000 concern grow into one capitalized at $2.5 million. He had seen its sales grow from $7,000 to $11.3 million a year, and saw its employees increase by a factor of 24, to 3,084.[34] "More, he had seen an unknown name, originally attached to a small line of hinges, become a world-famous trademark not only of builders' hardware but of steel, steel products, and byproducts." [35]

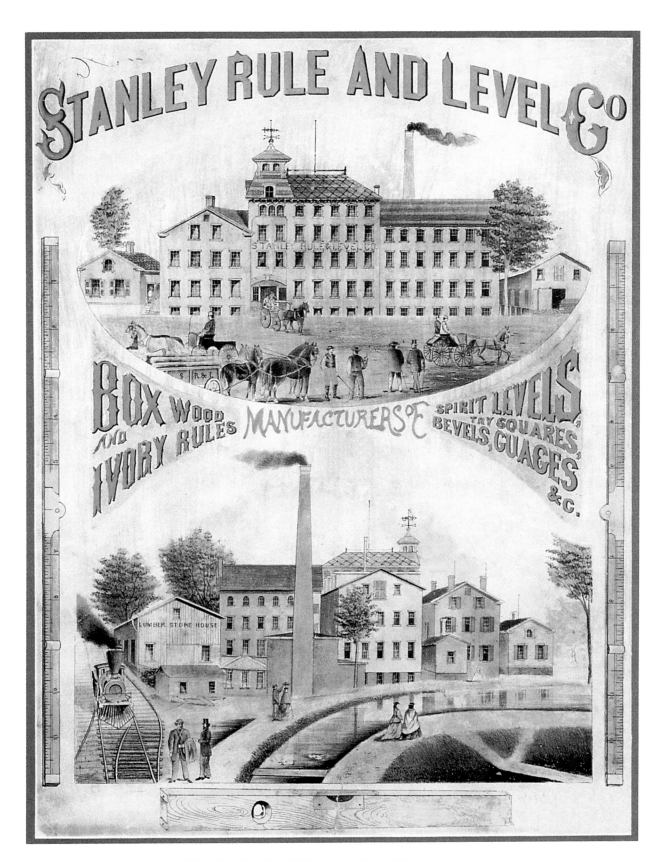

A broadside from the 1860s, reprinted in 1995 by John Walter.

CHAPTER SIX

THE STANLEY RULE & LEVEL COMPANY

"Many manufacturers today pattern their planes after the original 'Bailey Design.' But most of them have not mastered the kidney-shaped hole that makes the cap iron easier to adjust, or the single-piece Y-lever that won't spread when you advance the cutting iron, or the fully adjustable frog with a machined seat."

—— *Tool Traditions* catalog, 1995[1]

WHILE THE Stanley Works flourished, another company in New Britain, also named Stanley, was growing as well. It was the Stanley Rule & Level Company, established in 1857. Though the Stanley Rule & Level Company was smaller than The Stanley Works, it was renowned for the innovative and practical tools it manufactured and sold.

The Stanley Rule & Level Company was the result of a merger between two New Britain companies, Hall & Knapp, and A. Stanley & Company. Henry Stanley, a distant cousin of Frederick T. Stanley, was a silent partner in both businesses. Hall & Knapp, established in 1853 by Thomas S. Hall and Frederic Knapp, manufactured plumbs, levels, try squares, bevels and gauges. When the company was officially incorporated March 25, 1854, Henry Stanley became a shareholder. A. Stanley & Company was named for Henry's younger brother, Augustus, who established the company in October 1854 in a partnership with Henry, Gad and Timothy Stanley, as well as Thomas Conklin, a rule-maker and a former employee of Seymour & Churchill of Bristol, Connecticut. A. Stanley & Company purchased Seymour & Churchill, and began the manufacture of ivory and boxwood rules.

The company set up business in the top story of the J.B. Sargeant and Company factory building, owned by Henry Stanley.[2]

On July 1, 1857, the directors of both A. Stanley & Company and Hall & Knapp voted to combine the companies to form the Stanley Rule & Level Company, which was incorporated by an act of legislation in May 1858. The result was a joint stock company with capital of $50,000, and Henry Stanley as its first president.[3] The new Stanley Rule & Level Company, located on Elm Street in New Britain, manufactured a broad range of rules, levels, try squares and plumbs.

Henry Stanley was a shareholder or partner in many New Britain businesses, but, unlike William Hart, he was not interested in the day-to-day intricacies of running a company. "He was an organizer, a combiner and an enterpriser. He liked to put companies together, find good men to run them and stay out of everything in management except broad policy."[4]

Above: An illustration of the Stanley Rule & Level facilities in New Britain, Connecticut, as they appeared in 1868.

The Automation Poem

As early as the 1850s, automation was finding its way into the Stanley Rule & Level production process. Some employees were skeptical about the new techniques, as an 1857 employee poem indicates.

Improvements have been made, 'tis true.
To help the workmen as well as you,
But why must we, for all these, work
To pay the maker while he shirks.

There is one machine been made of late,
That does add greatly to our fate,
Across the bench it lengthwise lies,
And looks immortal to our eyes.

It is a curious thing we know,
And down to Barnum's it should go.
And there among his trinkets, stand
The work of your machinist's hands.[5]

Henry Stanley, a distant cousin of Frederick T. Stanley, founded the Stanley Rule & Level Company in 1857, and served as president until his death in May 1884. He was also president of The Stanley Works from August 1883 until his death.

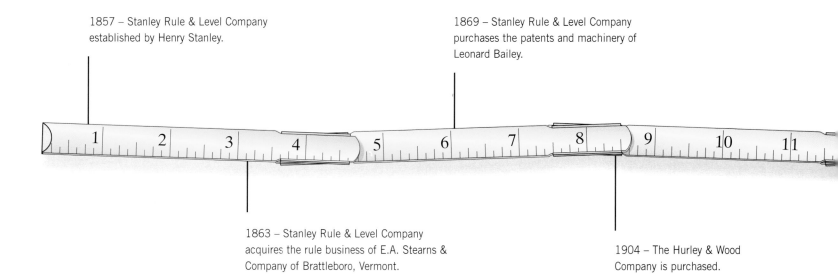

1857 – Stanley Rule & Level Company established by Henry Stanley.

1869 – Stanley Rule & Level Company purchases the patents and machinery of Leonard Bailey.

1863 – Stanley Rule & Level Company acquires the rule business of E.A. Stearns & Company of Brattleboro, Vermont.

1904 – The Hurley & Wood Company is purchased.

Novelty Items During the Civil War

To help the company stay in business during the Civil War, Henry Stanley began looking for other types of products to manufacture.[6] He purchased a tool-handle business owned jointly by Augustus Stanley and John Stanley, who were first cousins. The tool-handle business, which was already well-established, used hickory, rosewood and imported tropical hardwoods for its products.[7] Henry saw potential for these materials and expanded the company beyond tool handles to manufacture checkers, chessmen, blocks for use in schools, earrings, breast pins, brooches, sleeve buttons, drawer knobs, wooden toy pistols and handles for awls, chisels and hammers.[8]

On August 1, 1863, Henry Stanley acquired the rule business of E.A. Stearns & Company of Brattleboro, Vermont, a maker of top-quality, extremely accurate rulers.

Guy Dewey, William McNary and George Nichols, employees of the Ivory Rule Room at Stanley Rule & Level, in 1898.

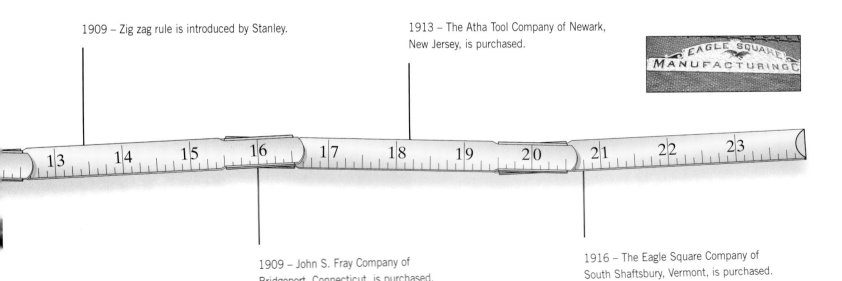

1909 – Zig zag rule is introduced by Stanley.

1913 – The Atha Tool Company of Newark, New Jersey, is purchased.

1909 – John S. Fray Company of Bridgeport, Connecticut, is purchased.

1916 – The Eagle Square Company of South Shaftsbury, Vermont, is purchased.

The Bailey Plane

While the Stanley Rule & Level Company was setting the industry standard for attractive, accurate and versatile rules, a company known as Bailey Chany & Company was winning respect in Boston for the quality of its planes, spokeshaves and scrapers. Though the company was only in business for one year, it was renowned for the plane invented by Leonard Bailey, which had several features that made it vastly superior to other planes on the market. The improvements were so important, yet so simple, that they are still used today on most bench planes manufactured by Stanley and its competitors.

Instead of a thick tapered blade that had to be set by hand between wedges, Bailey's plane utilized a thinner blade of constant thickness, in conjunction with a blade cap. This combination gave the blade the same rigidity as the thicker, tapered, blade, but was easier to manufacture from sheet stock. The durable blade was held securely in place so it wouldn't vibrate during use, and required less grinding than other blades. An additional feature allowed for a fine adjustment of the cutter, and prevented it from pushing backward and losing its setting during use.[16] "Leonard Bailey was a very colorful person," said Carl Stoutenberg in 1995. Stoutenberg is product line engineering manager and historian for The Stanley Tool Division. "He is the father of the plane as we know it today. He didn't invent the plane, but he made major improvements and had valuable patents."[17]

Though Bailey's plane was an engineering marvel, it did not achieve much success in the marketplace, apparently because Bailey had insufficient

A photograph of the Stanley Rule & Level Company Sound Money Club, taken outside the company offices during William McKinley's successful 1896 presidential campaign.

funds for adequate marketing and distribution.[18] On May 19, 1869, the Stanley Rule & Level Company purchased Bailey's machinery, existing inventory, and "parts in process" for $12,500.[19] The patents were acquired in a license agreement, the entire Bailey business was moved to New Britain, and Leonard Bailey was appointed superintendent of the plane factory. In early 1870, the Stanley Rule & Level Company announced a line of "Bailey's Patent Iron and Wood Bench Planes, Veneer Scrapers and Iron Spoke Shaves."[20]

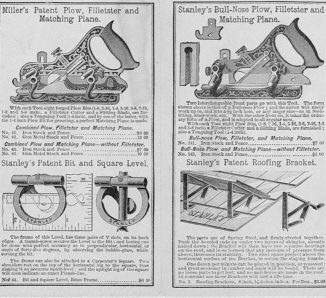

The Bailey plane was an immediate success, and, in 1871, the Stanley Rule & Level Company announced that more than 6,500 had been sold.[21] Even during the economic slump that crippled the nation between 1873 and 1878, sales of the Bailey plane continued to rise. In 1876, an astonishing 100,000 had been sold, and the following year, the number soared to 125,000.[22]

Bailey left the Stanley Rule & Level Company in 1875 following disputes over a royalty agreement, and started L. Bailey & Company in Hartford, Connecticut, where he began manufacturing a line of planes under the Victor name. He later sold this business to the Bailey Wringing Machine Company of Woonsocket, Rhode Island, which manufactured planes under the Defiance line patented by Joseph Bailey (no relation to Leonard Bailey) and improved by William H. Brown and David F. Williams. Leonard Bailey moved to Woonsocket to supervise the manufacture of both plane lines. Apparently, this new venture was not successful, because Bailey moved back to Hartford some time prior to 1880 and went to work manufacturing Victor planes and copy presses at the factory of the Hartford Screw Company.[23]

In January 1880, the Stanley Rule & Level Company purchased the Bailey Wringing Machine Company and also agreed to act as selling agents for Bailey's Victor line of planes. In July 1884,

Above: An 1888 catalog of carpenters' tools, featuring Bailey Planes and Miller's Patent Plows. Charles Miller worked for Stanley between 1872 and 1876, creating plows with distinctive, ornate frames.

Left: An iron plane from the price list above.

Stanley purchased the Victor business outright. From that point until his death in 1905, Bailey

JULY 1, 1874.

☞ OVER 70,000 PLANES NOW IN USE.

AWARDED

FIRST PREMIUM, SILVER MEDAL,

Cincinnati Industrial Exposition, October, 1870;

Auburn, N. Y., Industrial Association, March, 1871.

BAILEY'S PATENT

ADJUSTABLE

IRON AND WOOD

BENCH PLANES,

MANUFACTURED BY THE

STANLEY RULE AND LEVEL COMPANY,

New Britain, Conn.

Warerooms, 35 Chambers St., N. Y.

For Sale by all Hardware Dealers.

VICTOR PLANE
TRADE MARK
B

Center: Leonard Bailey sold his Victor line of adjustable planes and spokeshaves to Stanley in 1880.

Above: An 1874 pocket catalog featuring Leonard Bailey's award-winning bench planes. (Walter Jacob photograph/Charles and Walter Jacob collection.)

manufactured copy presses at a factory in Wethersfield, Connecticut.[24]

The Stanley Works still takes tremendous pride in the Bailey planes it continues to manufacture. *Tool Traditions*, a 1995 catalog of fine woodworking tools, noted that other companies have tried, without success, to copy the Bailey plane.

"Many manufacturers today pattern their planes after the original 'Bailey Design.' But most of them have not mastered the kidney-shaped hole that makes the cap iron easier to adjust, or the single-piece Y-lever that won't spread when you advance the cutting iron, or the fully adjustable frog with a machined seat.

"Stanley/Bailey bench planes also offer fully adjustable depth of cut, mouth opening and lateral position of the cutting iron, features essential to preventing blade chatter and chip clogging while you change from taking thick to tissue-thin shavings in hard or soft wood."[25]

The Contractor System

Between 1870 and 1900, the Stanley Rule & Level Company operated on a contractor system similar to the one in place at The Stanley Works. Contractors paid high per-piece rates for skilled craftsmen or highly trained machine operators, and gave their employees quite a bit of freedom, "on the theory that people on straight piecework were entitled to earn money or not, as they pleased."[26]

On pleasant days, it was common for an entire department to go outside and have a ball game. This angered people in other areas of the company, who were waiting for work from that department.[27] Contractors were known to allow beer-drinking on the job, even though accident reports clearly indicated that alcohol and safety did not mix.[28] The contractor days were described by a New Britain journalist in 1963.

"According to reports that have come down to present-day ears, contractors were an easygoing lot and tolerated practices that would horrify

today's foremen. For example, they permitted their employees to keep a bucket of beer at their elbow during working hours and looked the other way when errand boys entered the plant balancing on their shoulders poles from which were suspended pails of refreshment from the nearest saloon." [29]

Despite the obvious drawbacks of the contractor system, it encouraged higher efficiency and the development of new products.

Top: Visitors from the Lakota Sioux tribe of South Dakota look at a Stanley plane in front of company headquarters in 1911. This image was one of a series of posters that hardware merchants were encouraged to display to promote Stanley tools.

Above: This plane was an experimental model with a cast-brass frame. Production models did not have the patent information stamped on the wood.

"The contractors were master-craftsmen by origin, well trained and stubborn. And the mark of the craftsman is that he loves fine materials and fine workmanship for their own sakes; he is hipped on making things as well as they can be made — whether they need to be or not." [30]

In 1884, while serving as president of both The Stanley Works and the Stanley Rule & Level Company, Henry Stanley, who had been president of the Stanley Rule & Level Company since it was founded in 1857, passed away. He was succeeded by Charles Mead. [31] Fifteen years later, in 1899, Mead passed away and Henry's son, Frederick N. Stanley, was elected the company's new president. Frederick was known as "a man of admirable character and pleasant personality, generous, unassuming, genial and kindly." [32] In 1900, just one year after becoming president, Frederick passed away and former U.S. Patent Commissioner Charles E. Mitchell was elected president. Mitchell, a New York attorney who had been a director of the Stanley Rule & Level Company for several years, believed sincerely that product innovation was the key to success. [33]

The Industry Leader

By 1900, the Stanley Rule & Level Company was the largest maker of planes and related tools in the world, as well as the largest American manufacturer of rules, levels and similar marking devices used in the building trade. Inventors who worked for the Stanley Rule & Level Company were responsible for some of the most useful, beautiful and ingenious tools ever made. Justus A. Traut, for example, probably patented more tools than any other American tool inventor. Other renowned inventors included Charles

Left: A scratch awl from the 1902 Hurwood Tools catalog. Stanley Rule & Level purchased Hurley & Wood in 1904.

Below: A Hurwood machine screwdriver from the same catalog.

Miller, Christian Bodmer, Edmund A. Schade and Eppie J. McColloch. One of the more spectacular planes invented by Traut, Schade and McColloch was the Stanley No. 55 universal combination plane, which came with standard cutters and the option to purchase an additional 50 cutters. Manufactured and sold by Stanley between 1893 and 1960, it is considered one of the most useful but complicated planes ever manufactured.

By 1907, Stanley Rule & Level's sales had grown to nearly four times the volume of 1897. [34] Recognizing that this growth was partly due to development of the Canadian market, Stanley sought to establish a manufacturing facility there. Consequently, the company purchased the Roxton Tool & Mill Company of Quebec, and reorganized the plane-manufacturing plant to create a full factory for the Stanley Rule & Level Company. By 1920, the Roxton plant was able to manufacture four-fifths of the principal items distributed by its parent company. [35]

The Stanley Rule & Level Company was still a modest enterprise by today's standards, and it was run as such. All of the mail was opened by the treasurer, and all correspondence was handwritten. Office hours were 8 a.m. to noon and 1 to 6 p.m., every day but Sunday. No one in the office was permitted to smoke "except the manager, who rated the privilege of smoking fat Havana Seegars (sic) (with the bands on) not so much as a badge of dignity as to put visitors at their ease." [36]

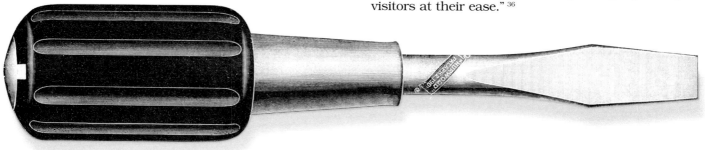

In 1908, the company abolished the contractor system and installed foremen to run the factories.[37] But even the foremen could not watch all employees at all times. A common problem during this period was the frequent employee usage of chewing tobacco. The difficulties associated with this habit were illuminated in the July 1917 minutes of the company's Operations Committee. "Mr. Cook stated this morning that a girl complained that as she was passing the packing room building on Church Street, someone spit tobacco juice out of one of our windows and soiled her shirt waist."[38] Shortly after the incident, a memo was distributed to management pertaining to the topic of, "Educating employees to use cuspidors and providing cuspidors throughout the factory."[39] The cost of installing one cuspidor for every three male employees in the entire plant was $375.

The dissolution of the contractor system led to increasing demands for workers' rights. By 1914, employees were covered by a Workman's Compensation Law.[40] Employees staged at least three successful walkouts in 1916, prompting the foremen to increase their hourly wages.[41]

Growth and Acquisition

When Charles Mitchell died in 1911, he was succeeded as president by Alix Stanley, the son of Frederick N. Stanley and grandson of Henry Stanley, and a man highly regarded within the ranks of the Stanley Rule & Level Company. Both Mitchell and Stanley believed in growth through acquisition, and in the two decades between 1900 and 1920, the Stanley Rule & Level Company purchased between 18 and 20 companies, expanding into the hand tools business by acquiring companies that manufactured hammers and other tools.

Among the first of these acquisitions was the American patent rights of the zig zag rule from a German company. This rule had brass hinges, so it could be unfolded as needed. The zig zag rule was first listed in the 1900 company catalog, and immediately sold well.[42]

When the Stanley Rule & Level Company decided to manufacture bit-braces, it acquired three small companies, the most significant of which was the John S. Fray Company of Bridgeport, Connecticut. Fray manufactured bit extensions, corner braces, ratchet braces and breast drills, while employing roughly 100 highly skilled people. The Stanley Rule & Level Company purchased Fray's business in 1909, and it became the Fray Division.[43] The company was subsequently moved to New Britain in 1924.

In 1904, the Stanley Rule & Level Company purchased the Hurley & Wood Company of Plantsville, Connecticut, a company known for its Hurwood line of tools, including a high-quality screwdriver, which featured a blade, shank and head all forged from one piece of steel. Stanley hired Hurley & Wood's co-owner, George E. Wood, who later patented a line of chisels that the company began to manufacture in 1913.

In 1906, the Stanley Rule & Level Company purchased the carpenter tool business of the Union Manufacturing Company of New Britain, and created the Union Plane Company. The success of zig zag rules and wooden tool handles prompted the Stanley Rule & Level Company to purchase the Harmon woodworking plant in Ashfield, Mass-

---

Right: An Atha No. 51½ Claw Hammer from 1919-1920. (Walter Jacob photograph/Charles & Walter Jacob collection.)

Left: A 6-inch Stanley/Fray Brace No. X3, manufactured between 1910 and 1918. The Stanley Rule & Level Company acquired Fray's business in 1909.(Walter Jacob photograph/Charles & Walter Jacob collection.)

achusetts, in 1910.[44] The following year, Stanley entered the vise marketplace by acquiring P. J. Leavens of Vineland, New Jersey, and moving the company to New Britain.[45]

In 1912, the Stanley Rule & Level Company purchased the hammer business of Humason & Beckley, an old New Britain company that was going out of business. But the acquisition proved disappointing, so in 1913, Stanley purchased the Atha Tool Company of Newark, New Jersey. Atha was a well-known maker of hammers, picks, hatchets, sledges, wedges, anvils, blacksmith's tongs, railroad track tools, cold chisels, punches and related items.[46]

In 1919, the Gage Tool Company of Vineland, New Jersey, was purchased.

The Eagle Square Company

Ever since the 1860s, the Stanley Rule & Level Company had been frustrated by its inability to manufacture a steel framing square. Company officers were reluctant to compete with the acknowledged master in the field — The Eagle Square Company of Vermont, founded in 1817 and emphatically not for sale.[47]

Carpenters valued these tools for their versatility and reliability, since they could measure both straight edges and angles. But the combination of right angles and rules made carpenter's squares a challenge to manufacture. "It was quite a process," admitted Francis Zambrello, current manager of the Eagle Square Plant in South Shaftsbury, Vermont. "Somewhere in the neighborhood of 24 different operations were required."[48] But after admiring the company for more than 20 years, the Stanley Rule & Level Company was finally able to purchase the Eagle Square Company in 1916. When Eagle Square came on the market, the Stanley Rule & Level Company jumped at the opportunity to acquire it. Not only did Eagle Square manufacture the sought-after carpenter's squares, but it also brought "a knowledge in woodworking that covered everything from sources of lumber supply, through methods of treatment, to cutting, milling, turning and finishing."[49]

The Stanley Works still manufactures carpenter's squares, but the process has been streamlined over the years, Zambrello said. "It's now somewhere around six operations," he said. "A big change."[50]

The Eagle Square Company is one of the few Stanley facilities that uses its own logo in concert with the Stanley logo. The 200,000-square-foot facility now manufactures aluminum levels, knives, T-squares

Above, right: A group of Stanley Rule & Level employees, photographed for a postcard in 1915. The names are handwritten on the back as follows: "Top Row — left to right. Boyer, Neuman, Young, Spaulding, T. Hazelwood, T. Diehl. Middle Row. R.M. Parsons, Flint, Nagle, Bodmer, A. Schade, Richards. Bottom Row. Johnson, Nuss, Coogan, G. Serf."

Above, center: A rare No. 58½ folding rule, loaded with so many scales and tables that there is no room for the Stanley trademark. (John Walter photograph.)

and chalk lines, among other products. "There are about 325 different products that run out of this facility," Zambrello said.[51]

World War I

During World War I, the Stanley Rule & Level Company manufactured large quantities of tools for use by the armed forces and in government construction. These tools included folding screwdrivers that could be used to assemble or repair guns, dental and surgeon's drills, and gas masks. Ninety-nine Stanley Rule & Level Company employees served in World War I, and two died in the conflict.

During the war, Stanley, along with most factories in the nation, faced a serious coal shortage. To save energy, management found it necessary to utilize only the engines that both ran machinery and propelled heat throughout the building.[52]

During this period, Stanley employees suffered an epidemic of influenza. At the height of the outbreak, on October 19, 1918, 284 employees, or 35 percent of the company's New Britain work force, were absent, and at least 10 employees succumbed to the disease.[53]

Following World War I, the Stanley Rule & Level Company surged back to full capacity, employing 1,600 people in six cities and towns of the United States and Canada.

By this time, the Stanley Rule & Level Company was as well-known by homeowners and carpenters as The Stanley Works was among builders, retail dealers, and distributors.[54] "It was partly this fact which moved the managements of the two companies to work out a merger in 1920.[55]

Above: Stanley acquired the American patent rights for zig zag rules, such as this 2-foot model, in 1909. (Walter Jacob photograph/Charles & Walter Jacob collection.)

Below: The Eagle Square Company, founded in South Shaftsbury, Vermont, as it appeared in about 1883. After admiring the company for decades, Stanley Rule & Level purchased it in 1916.

This dramatic photograph of two men suspended from the shaft of a Stanley hammer was used in advertisements during the thirties to demonstrate the unusual strength of Stanley tools.

CHAPTER SEVEN

JOINING FORCES

"This is to advise you that The Stanley Works has purchased the going manufacturing business of The Stanley Rule & Level Company. ... The present consolidation unites the manufacturing interests of the two Stanley companies that have grown side by side for almost 70 years, each developing its separate line of products for the Hardware Trade."

— 1920 Announcement[1]

BY 1920, Alix Stanley was considering retirement from Stanley Rule & Level, and he wished to sell his controlling interest in the company.[2] Other stockholders were willing to sell or merge with another company, as long as a few conditions were met. They did not want a tax penalty, they did not want jobs to be lost, and they did not want to jeopardize the excellent Stanley reputation.

The Stanley Works seemed like the ideal company to merge with Stanley Rule & Level. The two companies had been associated since they were started by distant relatives within the large Stanley family. Henry Stanley, a director of the Stanley Rule & Level Company, had served as the president of The Stanley Works. Alix Stanley was a director of The Stanley Works, and George Hart was a director of the Rule & Level. And perhaps the most compelling argument was that, within the hardware industry, Stanley was already perceived as one company.[3]

George Hart's brother, Walter, approached Alix Stanley while both were vacationing on Martha's Vineyard, off the coast of Massachusetts, during the summer of 1919. They discussed the merger, but "neither party would consider paying the large federal tax involved in the transfer of the shares, and the matter was definitely dropped."[4] Stanley Works President E.A. Moore, who strongly supported a merger or purchase of the Rule & Level, contacted his attorney, J. Earnest Cooper, to determine what strategies could be implemented to minimize the potential tax liability, as he later explained.

"We discussed the tax situation at length. Mr. Cooper finally, after repeated discussions with Mr. Stanley and myself, proposed the plan which was followed and was, as far as we knew, the first of its kind by which a large stockholder could dispose of his stock and avoid for a long time paying a federal tax on any possible profit. On this plan, The Stanley Works was to buy all the assets of the Stanley Rule & Level Company with an issue of preferred stock. An investment company was to be incorporated, called the Stanley Securities Company. A stockholder of the Stanley Rule & Level Company was to have the privilege of receiving all his proportion of the purchase price either in cash or in preferred shares of The Stanley Works, or in the shares of the Stanley Securities Company, or a portion of each as desired. This enabled the small stockholder to take payment in cash or hold his pre-

Above: A logo from *The Stanley Tool Guide*, published in 1935 by the Stanley Rule & Level plant. The 25¢ booklet offered advice on selecting and using chisels, saws and other tools.

ferred shares, and the large owner to hold his capital investment without tax, at the time, if he so desired. The plan, after a good deal of haggling by the principals over the price, was finally adopted and approved by the directors and stockholders of The Stanley Works and the Stanley Rule & Level Company." [5]

On May 1, 1920, The Stanley Works released an announcement of the merger, written by Moore.

"This is to advise you that The Stanley Works has purchased the going manufacturing business of the Stanley Rule & Level Company. The Stanley Works will now own and operate some twelve different plants and properties. ... The principal factories for the production of the finished product, and the main offices of the company, are in New Britain, Connecticut, but there are other factories located at Niles, Ohio; Newark, New

A 1923 counter display for Stanley's popular line of Four-Square tools. (Walter Jacob photograph/Charles and Walter Jacob collection.)

Jersey; Bridgewater, Massachusetts; South Shaftsbury, Vermont; Bridgeport, Connecticut; in Canada, at Hamilton, Ontario, and Roxton Pond; Quebec, and at Kobe, Japan. ... The present consolidation unites the manufacturing interests of the two Stanley companies that have grown side by side for almost 70 years, each developing its separate line of products for the Hardware Trade. ... This purchase should only tend toward a better and more complete development of the two businesses. Rightly consolidated, as we believe they are, they should be able to serve you better than when separate." [6]

The merger increased The Stanley Works' size by 50 percent, and added about $6 million in sales. It also added 1,252 employees, and further strengthened the Stanley name throughout the hardware and tool-making industries.[7]

Capitalization of The Stanley Works had increased from $2.5 million to $6.5 million between 1914 and 1920, with most of the revenues rep-

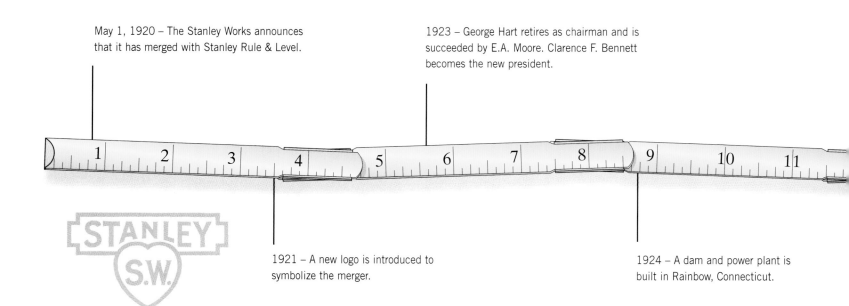

May 1, 1920 – The Stanley Works announces that it has merged with Stanley Rule & Level.

1923 – George Hart retires as chairman and is succeeded by E.A. Moore. Clarence F. Bennett becomes the new president.

1921 – A new logo is introduced to symbolize the merger.

1924 – A dam and power plant is built in Rainbow, Connecticut.

resented by increased earnings. Since the majority of capital from the Rule & Level merger had come from the exchange of stocks, The Stanley Works was left with considerable funds for investment.[8]

A Combined Strength

Deciding that The Stanley Works needed a new logo to symbolize the merger, the directors held a contest open to all Stanley employees. Winners W.L. Hagen and E.C. Hartman, who came up with nearly identical designs, both won cash prizes. The result was the "Sweetheart" trademark, combining the Rule & Level's notched rectangle with The Stanley Works' heart, adopted to honor former President William Hart.[9] Stanley products began carrying this logo in 1922.[10]

Right: Employees at The Stanley Works were given this 14-karat gold pin to celebrate 10 years with the company.

Far Right: This announcement appeared in *Popular Mechanics* in January 1921.

Our New Trade Mark!

STANLEY
S.W.

Announcement

WITH the purchase by The Stanley Works of The Stanley Rule and Level Company a new trade mark, as above shown, has been established. In the future it will be stamped upon dependable

Wrought Steel Hardware
and
Carpenters' Tools

which will be manufactured under the name

THE STANLEY WORKS

Main offices and plants: NEW BRITAIN, CONN.

Branch offices: NEW YORK   CHICAGO   SAN FRANCISCO   LOS ANGELES   SEATTLE

1925 – Stanley purchases the Tube and Stamping Company.

1929 – E.A. Moore retires.

1926 – Stanley purchases the Velbert Plant in Germany.

1930 – The "electric eye" door opener is introduced.

The Literary Digest for January 29, 1921

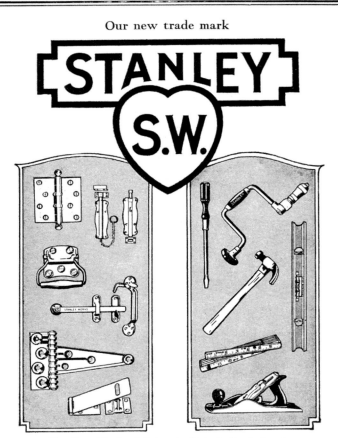

Our new trade mark

STANLEY
S.W.

Two Great National Industries Unite in Producing the Finest in Wrought Steel Hardware and Carpenters' Tools

BECOME acquainted with these dependable products. STANLEY Wrought Steel Butts, Hinges, Drawer Pulls, Bolts, Brackets, Screen and Garage Hardware, will be a constant source of satisfaction. Any architect is glad to specify them.

STANLEY Carpenters' Tools are first in the minds of good carpenters. The ownership of a STANLEY Hammer, Screw Driver, Plane, Rule, Level and Bit Brace will afford you many pleasing, profitable hours.

Catalogs of the above on request. Another STANLEY product is Storm Sash Hardware; ask your dealer to show it to you. Or, if more convenient, write us for folders B3.

THE STANLEY WORKS

Main offices and plant:
NEW BRITAIN, CONN.
Branch offices:
New York   Chicago   San Francisco   Los Angeles   Seattle
Atlanta

The directors of both companies agreed that combining the sales forces would increase efficiency. Each salesman would spend more time with distributors, selling both lines in less time than it would take for two men to visit. However, this plan did not succeed when put into practice. As it turned out, most salesmen had to meet with two separate buyers anyway to sell the different lines. Sales managers reverted to a system of having one salesman as an expert for each line.[11]

The new company continued the family atmosphere that had permeated both The Stanley Works and the Stanley Rule and Level Company. A 1921 issue of *The Stanley Workers* is filled with gossip, advice, bowling league scores and other indications that The Stanley Works was much more than simply a place to work. Matchmaking was common, with comments like: "Will you please tell me if Chris Bodmer is married?" A typical dispatch celebrates the light-hearted spirit of several employees. "Minnie and Gertie are getting to be sporty, enjoying box seats at the Lyceum when they attend that theater. What's the joke, girls, on the second conveyor? Laughter seems to be the general order of the day."[12]

In 1923, George Hart retired as chairman of The Stanley Works. He was succeeded in this post by E.A. Moore, while Clarence F. Bennett was elected the company's new president. "He was quite a guy," recalled Hoyt C. Pease, a retired executive vice president and board member. "Mr. Bennett lived almost right across the street from where my dad lived."[13]

During the early 1920s, The Stanley Works developed new strengths. This was a period of prosperity and national expansion, so demand was high for hardware, tools, steel and industrial products that had been difficult to obtain during World War I.

One of the first new lines produced by the consolidated interests was the Defiance line, acquired with the purchase of the Bailey Wringing Machine Company in 1880. Bailey had begun the line in 1875, and the first products manufactured by Stanley under the Defiance name were bench planes.[14]

In 1924, Stanley was able to loan its subsidiary, the Farmington River Power Company, more than $1 million for a new dam and power

Left: An advertisement in *The Literary Digest* of January 29, 1921.

plant in Rainbow, Connecticut. The new plant, just downstream from the old one, was finished by December 1925, and supplied current at 66,000 volts to New Britain. The *Hartford Daily Times* reported on the new plant shortly before construction was completed.

"The old water wheels along the Farmington River which once furnished power for saw mills and grist mills have long passed into oblivion, but rising in their stead stands the mighty dam and power plant of The Stanley Works of New Britain which is nearly completed at Rainbow. ... When this power station is fully completed it will be possible for anyone to close a small knife switch at some distant place and have the whole station start up and come onto the line ... The banging of solenoid-operated switches and the sparks of the relays together with the hum of the generators would furnish a thrill for anyone."[15]

In 1925, the Bridgeport steel mill, still known as the American Tube and Stamping Company, once again became available for purchase. By this time, The Stanley Works' need for steel had grown beyond the capacity of its Bridgewater, Massachusetts, plant, and Stanley finally purchased the company in 1926.[16]

To increase its wood supply, The Stanley Works acquired the Bryson Manufacturing Company woodworking plant, located in Pulaski, Tennessee. The purchase included 15,000 acres of hickory timber, which would be used for hammer handles.[17] The Pulaski plant is still in operation today.

The European Market

The Stanley Works developed a considerable export business during World War I, but, following the war, competition from Europe escalated. Stanley needed to manufacture goods in Europe that could compete with the low-priced European goods produced by poorly-paid European labor.[18] In 1925, Moore sent Bennett's right-hand man, Richard E. Pritchard, to Belgium to purchase land and plan construction of a plant in Antwerp. But before construction had begun, a German hardware manufacturer became available for purchase.[19] The plant, owned by Friedreich Carl von Bruck, and located in Velbert, Rhineland, had been

Clarence F. Bennett, president of The Stanley Works from 1923 to 1941, and chairman from 1941 to 1946.

in operation since the 1890s. It employed 600 people, and sold its products as far away as India and South Africa.[20] Bennett asked Pritchard to sell the Belgian property and, in 1926, The Stanley Works purchased the Velbert plant instead. John C. Cairns, one of Stanley's most promising young employees, was sent to Germany with a shipment of machinery and equipment to take charge of the new Stanley Works, GmbH.[21]

For some time, The Stanley Works had sought an overseas concern to manufacture hand tools. In 1937, Stanley purchased a controlling interest in the J.A. Chapman Limited firm in Sheffield, England, maker of steel and fine tools. The company, founded in the 1860s, was known for its excellent workmanship, highly skilled staff and able management.[22]

E.A. Moore Retires

When E.A. Moore retired in 1929, he sent a letter to the stockholders expressing his faith in the growing company.

An Electric Hammer

that needs no shock absorber

The improved mechanism of Stanley-Ajax Electric Hammers permits the tool to deliver powerful blows to the cutting tool without shock to the motor, the housing or the operator. This is an important feature which is appreciated by users everywhere.

They are unusually light and well balanced tools which can be operated in any position without "breaking the user's back."

Particularly useful in construction work for

drilling, chipping and channelling in either concrete, brick or stone. Also for chiseling wood or steel.

Equipped throughout with ball bearings. All parts of the mechanism are made of special alloy steels to insure durability.

No matter what the construction work may be, there are hundreds of jobs coming up every day where the Stanley-Ajax Hammer will save time and labor.

Send for full information. It will be worth your while to look into the savings that can be made with Stanley-Ajax Hammers.

[STANLEY]

THE STANLEY ELECTRIC TOOL CO.

New Britain, Conn.

Sales Offices and Service Stations: New York   Chicago   Cincinnati   Philadelphia   Detroit

STANLEY ELECTRIC TOOLS

DRILLS   HAMMERS   SAFETY SAWS   BENCH GRINDERS   SHEET METAL CUTTING TOOLS   SCREW DRIVERS   AERIAL GRINDERS

FOR ADVERTISERS' INDEX SEE NEXT TO LAST PAGE

The Stanley Works acquired four electric tool companies in 1929, including the Ajax Hammer Corporation, highlighted in this 1930 advertisement.

facturing Company of Cincinnati; the Ajax Hammer Corporation of New York; and the Unishear Company of New York. These acquisitions together became a division known as The Stanley Electric Tool Company, which manufactured electric shapers, routers, stone and wood saws, and metal cutting shears.[32]

Despite the sound purchases of the late 1920s, sales during the Depression were understandably slow. The 1930 Annual Report stated, "In 1930 sales of all divisions were 35 percent below the sales in 1929. Because of lessened business, we have been compelled to run our plants on reduced schedules with reduced working forces. We have made no general reduction of wages, but have felt it necessary and just to make a reduction in the compensation of all of our salaried employees."[33] But by 1932, the tool business began to pick up again, partly because Americans couldn't afford professional contractors, and so learned how to perform home repairs themselves.[34]

Lasting Innovations

In 1930, the company introduced the incredible "electric eye" door opener, which seemed to magically open a door as a person approached. Stanley's revolutionary Magic Door was first installed at the Wilcox Pier Restaurant in Savin Rock, Connecticut. The product gained national attention later that year when one was installed in the Pennsylvania Station railroad terminal in New York City. The door, "which functioned automatically in obedience to the signal of a photoelectric cell, or 'magic eye,' whenever a person approached," was soon a standard feature in factories, hospitals, banks, travel terminals, restaurants, hotels and other high-traffic areas.[35] A *New York Times* article in 1955 praised the innovation. "Ali Baba had to say 'Open Sesame' to move the magic door to the cave of the forty thieves. Today's Magic Doors don't even require that much effort."[36]

In December 1931, The Stanley Works introduced another product that would have a lasting positive impact on the company. Hiram Farrand of Berlin, New Hampshire, had invented a coilable steel rule, known as the "push-pull," "flexible rigid," or "concave-convex" rule. Farrand had marketed the product as the "Farrand Rapid Rule," but didn't experience much success, probably because he lacked the necessary financial resources and business acumen to distribute his novel rules. The Stanley Works purchased the business, and acquired Farrand's important patent regarding the cross curvature of the steel ruler blades. Unlike other tape rules, which were floppy and limp, Farrand's rules stood out rigidly, yet could still be coiled.

"By giving a rule standout, there now was a measuring device of 6 or 8 feet, which could coil up and fit in one's pocket," explained Carl Stoutenberg, unofficial historian of the Stanley Tools Division. "This spelled ultimate doom for the folding wood rules. The Farrand blade patent ranks up there with the Bailey plane patents and the later 1963 Powerlock rule patent as probably the most valuable patents the Stanley Hand Tools Division has ever owned."[37]

Unlike the popular zig zag rule, the tape rule had an automatic spring that allowed the user to easily extend or retract the blade, and a compact case that made it easy to hold and use. A hook on one end of the ruler allowed the user to clip it to one end of the item being measured. The zig zag, on the other hand, had to be unfolded with two hands, was bulky to carry, and lacked the hook.

In 1932, a line of Roll-Up and Swing-Up garage doors was introduced to take advantage of the growing number of automobile owners in the United States. Within a year after its introduction, this new line was justifying itself and giving promise of outdistancing the older line of garage hardware.[38]

A New Symbol for a Changing Company

In 1934, directors of The Stanley Works opted to change the company's logo from the sweetheart design to something more modern. After twelve years, some of the magic had rubbed off William H. Hart's name, and it was felt that a simpler trademark would be better suited for representing the increasingly broad line of products made by The Stanley Works.[39] The resulting trademark, which simply depicts the word "Stanley" within a notched rectangle, is still stamped on

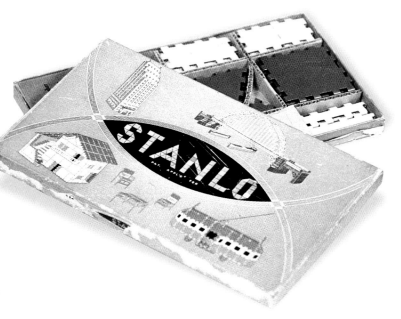

Above: During the 1930s, Stanley manufactured Stanlo, a toy set featuring metallic pieces of varying sizes that could be dovetailed together with pins. Larger sets included an electric motor to power the more elaborate constructions.

Left: A 6-foot Farrand tape rule from 1930, the year before The Stanley Works acquired the important Farrand patents.

Stanley products today. Company officers also felt that the Rule & Level Plant was not a sufficient name to describe Stanley's many tool manufacturers throughout the world, so in 1937, the name was changed to the Stanley Tools Division of The Stanley Works.[40]

The cover of *Time*, August 2, 1954. Stanley rapidly became an industry leader in the booming Do-It-Yourself market.

CHAPTER EIGHT

WORLD WAR II AND THE POST-WAR BOOM

"This war, which is not of our choosing, seems certain to be long and hard and all will be called upon for sacrifice in one form or another. Employees not called to service in the country's armed forces have a duty to render toward early and successful ending of the war, working to produce materials needed in defense of the country."

— Richard E. Pritchard[1]

EVEN BEFORE WORLD War II officially began with Germany's invasion of Poland in 1939, executives at The Stanley Works knew that its German facility was in peril. If the factory was either destroyed or confiscated by the increasingly powerful Nazi regime, the Stanley investment would be worthless. Recognizing this possibility, the company simply wrote off the subsidiary at its full $600,000 book value. The Stanley Works treated the facility as though it ceased to exist, and operations ground to a halt in 1939. Though the facility was bombed by allied aircraft twice in 1945, it remained standing and was restored in 1950.[2]

Stanley's facility in Sheffield, England, was in the process of adding several new buildings when the war began, and it quickly converted to war production. Hoyt C. Pease, who had been dispatched to Sheffield in 1937, three years after he graduated from Yale and joined The Stanley Works, offered one theory of why the facility survived the war. "The story goes that the Germans were so sure they were going to take England with no problem at all that when they bombed Sheffield they never bombed any of the steel plants," he said. "They wanted to keep it, so that when they arrived, they would have a steel mill."[3]

The United States did not officially join the fighting until the December 7, 1941 Japanese attack on Pearl Harbor, which killed 2,403 Americans and destroyed 19 ships and 150 aircraft. Within four days, the United States declared war on Japan and her Axis partners, Italy and Germany.

By that time, American industries had already been re-tooled and were contributing vigorously to the effort. The Stanley Works stepped up production so it could supply the government with such products as hand and electric tools, hardware, steel strapping and stamped metal parts. The Stanley Works also provided tools that helped construct new manufacturing facilities, and, most important of all, produced steel for government use, providing a valued material that was in short supply.[4]

To accelerate wartime production, The Stanley Works added new production facilities and hired additional workers to produce hundreds of tons of war munitions, including nearly 1.7 billion steel cups for the manufacture of .30-caliber tracer ammunition; 460 million belt-links which, when assembled with .50-caliber cartridges, formed the chain-belts in which the rapid fire ammunition was

Above: A Stanley Hobby House tool set from the fifties.

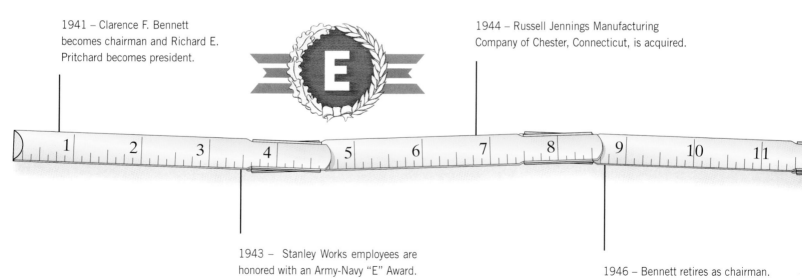

1941 – Clarence F. Bennett becomes chairman and Richard E. Pritchard becomes president.

1944 – Russell Jennings Manufacturing Company of Chester, Connecticut, is acquired.

1943 – Stanley Works employees are honored with an Army-Navy "E" Award.

1946 – Bennett retires as chairman.

fed through machine guns; 36 million cartridge clips for .30-caliber M1 rifle ammunition; clips for Browning automatic rifles; 5 million magazines for the .30-caliber carbine; metal gas mask parts; fins for guiding bombs in flight; parts for parachute flares; buckles for aircraft windshield de-icers; ammunition box hinges and hasps; and variable condensers for aircraft and ship radios.[5]

The Stanley Works was guided through World War II by new leadership. C.F. Bennett had retired from the presidency in 1941, leaving the post he had held since 1923. He became chairman of the board until 1946, when he retired following 50 years of employment at The Stanley Works. Richard E. Pritchard, who had joined The Stanley Works in 1914 after graduating from Dartmouth College, succeeded Bennett as president. "He was someone I had great respect for," said Donald Davis, who was hired as assistant manager of labor relations in 1948, and who would become president in 1966 and CEO in 1977. "He was a superb individual and business leader in my opinion."[6]

John Cairns, who had set up Stanley's factory in Velbert, Germany, in 1926, became a vice president.[7]

Left: The Stanley Works GmbH in Velbert, Germany, in 1951. Because of the war, the plant was closed between 1939 and 1950.

"John Cairns epitomized to me a Yankee business-man," said Ronald Gilrain, who was hired as marketing manager of Stanley Tools in 1960 and retired in 1993 as vice president of public affairs and marketing. "He was very calm, very objective. He had a vision of growth inside and outside the United States."[8]

To boost morale, The Stanley Works held a contest for its employees to invent a war slogan. There were 800 entries, and Ethel Rodin and Anthony Scarfe proposed the identical slogan, "We're In It — Let's Win It," without collaborating. Each won a $50 war bond.[9] Second prize of a $25 war bond was awarded to Charles Fromer, for the slogan "No Job's Done until We've Won."[10]

The July 1941 issue of *The Stanley World*, formerly known as *The Stanley Workers*, was filled with news of employees who were serving in the war. As usual, the employees of The Stanley Works demonstrated good humor, even when confronted with the seriousness of war. "Thus far our vivacious little Alma has lost four boy friends due to the draft," noted one item in the newsletter. Stanley employees were always encouraged to voice their opinions and concerns about the company, and to suggest improvements. The same issue of *The Stanley World* featured a list of employees who received cash awards as high as $100 for making suggestions on how to improve operations.[11]

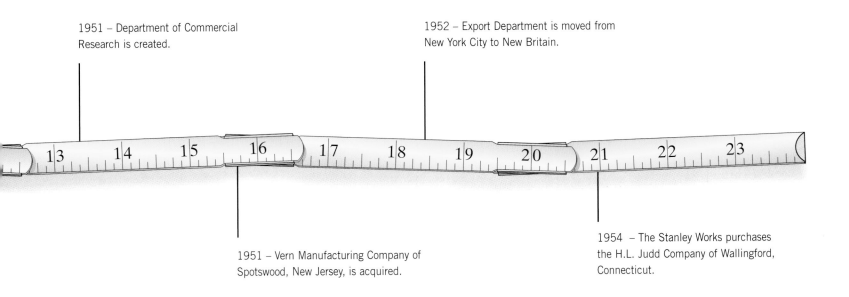

1951 – Department of Commercial Research is created.

1952 – Export Department is moved from New York City to New Britain.

1951 – Vern Manufacturing Company of Spotswood, New Jersey, is acquired.

1954 – The Stanley Works purchases the H.L. Judd Company of Wallingford, Connecticut.

Because of the hard work of employees, The Stanley Works won a series of coveted Army-Navy "E" Awards for outstanding achievement in the production of war equipment. Many American companies won "E" Awards during World War II, but Stanley was honored not only for the company as a whole, but for its individual divisions as well. The Steel Division won three pennants, and additional pennants were awarded to Stanley Tools in New Britain, the Eagle Square facility in Vermont, the Atha facility in New Jersey, the Pulaski woodworking plant in Tennessee, and the Harmon woodworking plant in Ashfield, Massachusetts.[12]

Recipients were given a pennant for each plant, and pins for all employees in the plants so honored. Companies that won the "E" Award proved that their work was exceptional in both quality and quantity. Other qualities shared by "E" Award winners were low absentee rates, an ability to overcome wartime production obstacles, and effective training of the new employees hired to replace workers who had gone to war.

In January 1943, more than 3,000 employees attended a ceremony in their honor, which featured speeches from Connecticut Governor Raymond Baldwin, New Britain Mayor George Quigley, and Army Colonel C.E. Snow. President Pritchard accepted the "E" Award, and expressed his appreciation for the great honor.

"This tribute of the nation to the efforts of the men and women of The Stanley Works comes to us in the year of our 100th anniversary. Nothing we have accomplished in the past century has given us more gratification than this recognition for having done our job well thus far, in the hour of our nation's greatest need. One of our employees has summed up the policy which has been and will continue to be our guiding principle: 'We're In It — Let's Win It!'"[13]

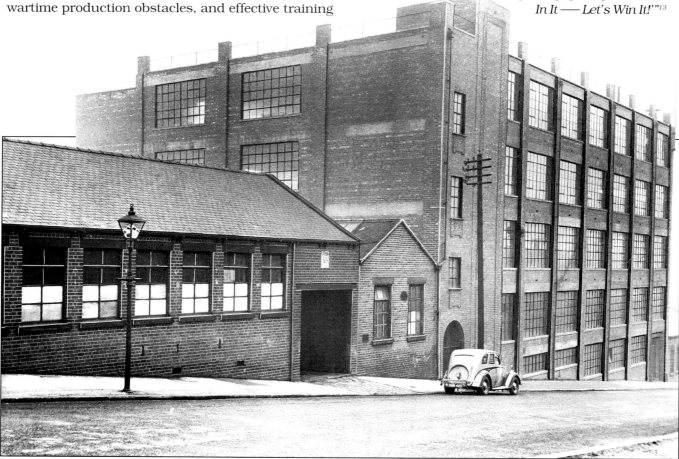

Stanley's Sheffield, England, plant in 1939.

Helping to win the war more directly were the 1,285 Stanley men and women who joined the armed services. Many were decorated for valor in action, and 44 gave their lives in service to their country.[14]

Post-War Growth

When the war ended in 1945, The Stanley Works experienced a surge in sales and production. By 1946, the sales department alone had more than doubled in size over pre-war staffing levels, and the company scrambled to hire new workers to fill jobs that were continually created.[15] In a 1945 interview with the *New Britain Herald*, Pritchard said he expected the growth to continue.

"We anticipate a period of countrywide building construction and there is an accumulated export demand for our products which could not be adequately taken care of during wartimes. Both of these considerations, as well as others, should keep us very busy for some time to come."[16]

Pritchard was correct. Between 1945 and 1950, Stanley sales increased from $36.6 million to $76.5 million, and profits more than tripled, from $1.8 million to $5.9 million. A backlog of orders put on hold during the war provided one source for growth, but those orders were filled within a year. A more significant explanation for Stanley's rapid growth was a baby boom that dramatically increased the American population. Stanley tools and hardware helped build the homes, shopping centers and office buildings for the new suburbs sprouting up outside American cities. As the nation's standard of living

Above: Richard E. Pritchard, president of The Stanley Works from 1941 to 1950, and chairman of the board from 1950 to 1955.

Left: President Richard E. Pritchard and Stanley employee Charles P. Wainright proudly display one of the Army-Navy "E" flags awarded to The Stanley Works during World War II.

rose, Americans purchased an unprecedented number of automobiles and electric appliances, creating a seemingly insatiable demand for steel, pressed parts and strapping.[17]

The Fifties

The decade of the 1950s ushered in still more Stanley acquisitions and expansion, as well as new leadership. In 1950, Richard E. Pritchard was elected Stanley's chairman of the board, and John C. Cairns became the company's new president.[18]

John C. Cairns was president of The Stanley Works from 1950 to 1961, and chairman of the board from 1961 to 1966.

in the floor, caused a door to close very slowly. It was one of the few hinges that The Stanley Works did not manufacture. The second product was an automatic door operator, controlled by a plastic mat on the floor, as opposed to Stanley's traditional line of automatic doors, which were operated by a photoelectric cell. The Vern door operator was subsequently added to the Magic Door line in the Hardware Division.[34]

By 1952, the Bridgeport Steel Mill had become obsolete.[35] Stanley directors wanted to modernize the plant instead of shutting it down, but doing so would be prohibitively expensive. The officers joined with a group of investors who had been trying to start a mill from scratch, and together they created The Northeastern Steel Corporation. The investors raised $15 million in capital and purchased the mill from The Stanley Works for $1 million.[36] The mill was updated from its 188,000-ton capacity to a 300,000-ton capacity, and its officers announced that it would supply steel to companies throughout New England.

In 1954, The Stanley Works purchased the H.L. Judd Company of Wallingford, Connecticut. The company, which became known as the Stanley-Judd Division, made drapery and household metal hardware.[37] The following year, Stanley acquired the Denison Corporation of North Miami, Florida, for $1.3 million, a company that manufactured aluminum window awnings and aluminum jalousie windows and doors.[38] President Cairns voiced his pleasure with the acquisition, noting that, "It is estimated that the aluminum window business is worth $250 million, and while Stanley's part is currently small, the opportunity for growth in it is great." The division was later renamed Stanley Building Specialties.[39]

Do-It-Yourself

In the early 1950s, a phenomenon swept the country that brought tremendous opportunity to The Stanley Works and other tool companies: the Do-It-Yourself trend. In 1954, *Time* magazine published a cover story titled "Do-It-Yourself — The New Billion-Dollar Hobby."

"In the postwar decade, the Do-It-Yourself craze has become a national phenomenon. The once indispensable handyman who could fix a chair, hang a door or patch a concrete walk has been replaced by millions of amateur hobbyists who do all his work — and much more — in their spare time and find it wonderful fun. In the process, they have turned Do-It-Yourself into the biggest of all U.S. hobbies and a booming $6 billion-a-year business. ... In the Do-It-Yourself cult are such big-wigs as U.S. Steel Vice President David Austin, who has a two-room, $5,000 wood-working workshop packed into his Pittsburgh apartment; former Secretary of State Dean Acheson, who makes his own furniture; TV and radio luminaries Desi Arnaz, Edgar Bergen and Fibber McGee, who spend their spare time puttering around with shelves and kitchen cabinets; movie and recording stars George Montgomery, Perry Como, Dan Duryea and Jane Russell, who do their own handiwork, build boats and furniture.

The Surform shaper was one of the most innovative products ever introduced by The Stanley Works. The versatile tool could shape, smooth, trim and cut a variety of materials, from wood to mild steel. With no blades to sharpen and nothing to adjust, it was easy for even the most amateur Do-It-Yourselfer to use.

"For many Americans, Do-It-Yourself makes possible luxuries that once existed only in their dreams. ... Says one Do-It-Yourselfer: 'A $1.25-an-hour bookkeeper is not going to pay a $3.50-an-hour carpenter very long.' ... And the therapeutic value of Do-It-Yourself is hard to overestimate. ... A harried executive who took up woodworking in his spare hours to ease the tension swears it kept him from suicide.

"In the fast-growing market, the fastest-growing business of all is in the basic machines for the Do-It-Yourself workshop. Before the war, the power tool industry rarely topped $25 million in sales; now it is a $200 million business, with a 25 percent increase predicted for 1954, and its products are America's most popular gadgets. Old companies in the field have suddenly come to life, and dozens of new ones have popped up."[40]

The Stanley Works was ideally positioned to benefit from this national trend, and it quickly developed products for this new market. In its 1953 Annual Report, the company discussed several ideas for keeping up with the increasing demand for Do-It-Yourself products.

"Promotion of our hardware and tools sales has sought to take full advantage of the current "Do-It-Yourself" vogue and the growing importance of the "Home Workshop" idea. In Hardware lines, the continued large-scale building of single-family homes has prompted the Hardware Division to concentrate attention on such lines as household hardware, rustic iron hardware and sliding door hardware. We have also developed a new line of Ranchcraft hardware inspired by the popular ranch-type home."[41]

By 1955, The Stanley Works enjoyed the highest sales in its 113-year history, with sales of nearly $92.5 million and net earnings of $5.6 million. The following year, despite a sharp decline in residential construction, sales rose to $98.8 million.[42]

In 1955, Pritchard retired as the chairman of the board after 41 years with The Stanley Works. A *New Britain Herald* editorial expressed the community's respect for the departing chairman.

Above: A Stanley Tools advertisement featuring Ricardo Montalban and his son, Mark. This 1958 ad is an example of the company's growing focus on the Do-It-Yourself market.

"The unexpected retirement of Richard E. Pritchard as chairman of the board of The Stanley Works will leave a tremendous void in the industrial leadership of this community. ... It can be truly said that he is a man whose astute leadership contributed immensely to the firm which he headed. Throughout his 14 years as board chairman at Stanley Works, he guided the firm to double the volume of business it enjoyed when he took over."[43]

The following year, E. Allen Moore passed away at the age of 91. His obituary described him as "a good friend, a captain of industry, a poet, a philosopher and a philanthropist."[44]

Until Cairns became chairman in 1961, the post was left vacant and Cairns was the leader of the company in fact, if not in title. Cairns strongly believed in market research, and in 1954 he developed the Department of Long Range Planning in order to help division managers understand their specialized markets. Cairns explained the importance of the new department in a 1960 *Stanley World* article that looked back at some of the developments of the fifties.

"Certain luxuries of the past, such as plenty of time and second chances, could no longer be afforded. ... It became apparent that long range

plans would be necessary, if performance were to be accomplished within an acceptable time limit. ... The benefits of the action have been most noticeable. More and more, thoroughly worked out plans are being accomplished on schedule. Standards of performance, whether in the factory or in marketing and sales, are being raised and attained, standards which are absolutely essential to maintain Stanley's market position against competition."[45]

In 1956, a Marketing Department was established to guide the Sales Department and handle advertising and merchandising. Sales were bolstered by new marketing techniques, including the Profitool display program introduced by Stanley Tools General Manager Ken Freedell in 1956. Profitool increased turnover by displaying popular hand tool items, encouraging browsing and impulse purchases. It included a basic stock guide and blueprinted program complete with displays and ticket prices.

Prior to such display innovations, tools were generally stored on shelves behind the counters of hardware stores. Customers would ask for specific items, which the merchants would bring to the counter. Profitool, which took more than two years to develop, was an immediate success across the country.

Ken Freedell, general manager of Stanley Tools, stands in front of a Profitool display.

Steel Strikes of the Fifties

In 1952, the steel division of The Stanley Works was one of many steel manufacturers throughout the nation taken over by the United States government in an effort to avert a nationwide strike by the United Steel Workers. In Stanley's case, the government took control of the Bridgeport mill.[46]

Continued nationwide steel industry strikes managed to affect operations at The Stanley Works. "Two of them, in 1954 and in 1959, hurt us badly," Cairns said. "We lost business in 1954, and in the shutdown of 1959, after we had exhausted our very large inventory."[47]

Despite these setbacks, Stanley remained committed to its philosophy of teamwork. Many outside observers credited Cairns with averting more serious union problems by hiring and promoting qualified personnel. A stock recommendation by Putnam & Company in 1961 paid tribute to Cairns' management skills and the spirit of togetherness that has always been a Stanley tradition.

"The 1950s experienced relative peace from crippling dissension between those in unions and the management group. It is the best proof of a common desire for a strong future for Stanley. It shows a respect for the importance of each employee's job and the responsibility that each job carries. It has reflected a spirit of teamwork which is bound to earn a high place for the company and the promise of a stable future for all employees, as it is continued into the future."[48]

Planning for the Future

The same Putnam report noted that one key to Stanley's success was the company's ability to plan for the future.

"The year 1955 marked the turning point in Stanley's management philosophy. In that year President John C. Cairns, who recognized the problems that were building up for the company, started to update both management and operations. Where individual divisions had been nearly autonomous in the past, Mr. Cairns began to build a centralized line and staff management organi-

zation and systematically attack the problems of product development, manufacturing methods, distribution and marketing. He promoted from within the company and brought men in from the outside. This program gathered momentum as it progressed and was accompanied by similar changes at the division level. Simultaneously Stanley set out to map a course for the future."[49]

As part of the expansion described in the report, The Stanley Works invested $3 million in 1955 to expand its Steel Division in New Britain. The new factory, which employed 343, boasted a production increase of about 40 percent.[50] In 1957, a new $2.5 million Steel Strapping Division factory was completed, with 100,000 square feet of manufacturing space and 37,500 square feet of office space.[51] By 1959, The Stanley Works was shipping 50 percent more strapping than it had shipped in 1956.[52]

Part of the expansion process called for Stanley to improve its technological capabilities. In 1956, an "electric brain" was installed at the company, in reality an accounting machine that served to speed up payroll and stock control operations. The *New Britain Herald* described it as "the first calculator of its type to be installed by a manufacturing concern in this area."[53] The company installed a private branch exchange telephone system in 1955, heralded as "the largest in the New Britain area with a capacity of 800 individual lines."[54] And in 1957, an electroplating machine was installed at the Hardware Division, weighing in at 110 tons and capable of plating 100 racks of components per hour.[55]

To eliminate overlapping efforts, the Pressed Metal Division was combined with the Hardware Division in 1958. The three principal sections of the new Hardware Division were Builders' Hardware, Industrial Hardware and Magic Door.[56]

In the late fifties, two new plants were added to The Stanley Works, Great Britain, Ltd. The new British factories, which were located in Cardiff, Wales, and Ecclesfield, England, manufactured hammers, carpenter's planes, Yankee tools, push-pull rules, knives and shapers.[57] The importance of Stanley's presence in the United Kingdom was acknowledged in the company's 1957 Annual Report. "We would have been forced out of many hand tool world markets in recent years were it not for our production at Sheffield."[58]

Stanley's steel mill at 65 Burritt Street increased the company's steel production by about 40 percent when it opened in 1955, and played a critical role in the company's worldwide expansion during the sixties.

CHAPTER NINE

WORLDWIDE GROWTH

"Surveys indicate that the Stanley name, in the minds of the individual and industrial consumer, stands for a high degree of product excellence."

— Securities distributor Blyth & Company, 1962[1]

T HE STANLEY WORKS began the decade by improving its popular tape rule. In 1960, the company began coating the rule blade with Mylar, a Du Pont-trademarked polyester film that dramatically improved the life of the blade. "The amazing new miracle plastic covers every inch of Stanley's new LIFE GUARD rule blades, safeguards against solvents, oil, alkalis, acids — practically anything!" enthused an advertisement that appeared in *Hardware Age*, *Hardware Retailer* and *Building Supply News* in 1960. "Rugged? You bet! This new blade withstood more than 10,000 passes with an abrasive eraser — without affecting legibility."[2]

A 1960 press release also touted the new black-on-yellow coloring of the blade. "This color is no gimmick. Scientific studies by leading highway safety experts confirm that yellow offers the most contrast of any color — and can be distinguished the greatest distance in any light."[3]

A few years later, in 1963, Stanley would introduce the revolutionary Powerlock, a product that instantly set the industry standard. Equipped with a convenient thumb-activated locking mechanism, the Powerlock proved so successful that it made other rules virtually obsolete. Francis Zambrello, manager of the Eagle Square plant in Vermont, said in a 1995 interview that the facility stopped making folding wooden rules because "the volume really dropped.

Powerlock rules are what everybody buys now," he said.[4]

As always, The Stanley Works developed and introduced new items. In 1960, the Steel Division added precoated steel to its line.[5] To keep up with demand for its expanding line of products, the company built a new $1.8-million woodworking plant in Pulaski, Tennessee to replace its 54-year-old wood processing mill.[6]

As part of the ongoing effort of President John Cairns to streamline company operations, the Russell Jennings Manufacturing Company was dissolved, and its tools and equipment were consolidated in the New Britain and Sheffield plants. Also, Stanley-Humason became a Stanley Works division called Stanley Industrial Components.[7]

Stanley continued to expand its presence in England in 1960, when it purchased S.N. Bridges & Company, Ltd., of London, among the largest British manufacturers of electric and pneumatic power tools.[8] Despite these expansion efforts, a national economic decline in 1960 caused a $10 million drop in sales, from $105.7 million in 1959 to $95.4 million in 1960.

Above: This 1960 van allowed salesmen to drive from dealer to dealer selling products.

On The Road With Stanley

The Stanley Works first took to the road in 1937, when it stocked a double trailer with hundreds of Stanley products and visited hardware stores across the country. "It has always been the desire of The Stanley Works to find a means of showing all their customers the complete line of Stanley products," explained the *Stanley News.*

"Hundreds of items are displayed in this coach. Some are integral parts of it while others are mounted on display boards. Even a working model of the Magic Door is included in this display. Most likely there are items in this coach which you have not yet seen, items which you can readily sell. Having only one of these coaches on the road, it will be some time before it makes a circuit of the country. But when it does arrive in your town be sure your complete staff visits it. Hundreds are visiting it daily and many are astonished at the little less than one thousand items displayed, all manufactured by Stanley."[14]

In 1949, the bus grew into a fleet of Rollorama coaches, each carrying more than 1,300 sample items to retailers. The 1953 bus (below) commemorated 100 years since the beginning of Stanley Tools.

engineers had developed, Stanley began researching what customers wanted, and then having new-product engineers fill those needs. Executives credit C. Kenneth Freedell, executive vice president and general manager of Stanley Tools, with steering the company in this new direction. "He kind of transformed the company," said Richard Hastings, himself president and general manager of Stanley Tools from 1966 to 1980. "He moved it from a manufacturing-driven company to a market-driven company."[15]

C. Kenneth Freedell, executive vice president and general manager of Stanley Tools, led the company away from a manufacturing-driven philosophy and toward a market-driven one.

Among Freedell's innovations was the Uni-Rack display, introduced in 1962, which allowed retailers to showcase an assortment of Stanley tools. Stanley vans equipped with the displays traveled the country, showing retailers how Uni-Racks would look in their stores.

Another lasting innovation was carding, a packaging system in which tools and hardware were affixed to cardboard backing and covered with plastic. "In the old days, everything was in a box," said Hoyt Pease, who has since retired as executive vice president. "I think you can give Ken credit for putting it on a card where people could see it or feel it."

"When the products were in boxes, if you wanted to get a scratch awl, you would go to the store and the merchant would take it out of the box, and you'd get a scratch awl. That's all you would buy because you weren't looking for anything else. There were no displays. Today, when you go to a store, there are all these things that suggest that instead of a scratch awl, maybe you'd like to get a nice screwdriver and a nice hammer and maybe something else as well."[16]

Davis discussed the new focus of The Stanley Works in a 1965 speech before the National Retail Hardware Association Congress.

"We have now learned that being market-oriented or customer-minded is no longer enough. We must be market-involved and customer-involved. ... We must make what field studies demonstrate our customers need, rather than what we have profitably made in the past."[17]

The evolving philosophy at The Stanley Works was noticed throughout the hardware industry, as well as by stock brokerage houses. In a 1964 stock recommendation, Putnam & Company lauded The Stanley Works for its management style, which gave advancement opportunities to a large number of employees.

"When John C. Cairns became chief executive in 1955, the need to decentralize and revitalize management was subsequently given top priority. Since then, certain outsiders have been hired to fill key executive positions. Equally significant, a large number of employees have been promoted upward and across the large, 8,400-man company. Along with concerted efforts to upgrade information flow among all departments and divisions, basic attitudes have been sharpened functionally, i.e. in marketing, production, engineering, research and accounting. Increased profitability

and planned growth are the basic objectives. ... The departure in 1962 of Howard Richardson, who was elected president early in 1961 ... was viewed as a body blow to the company's progress. This is largely mythical — the 'blow' was unexpectedly poorer earnings in 1962 in a better year for the economy than in 1961. ... Middle management is considered to be much stronger than it was three to five years ago."[18]

Donald W. Davis was hired by The Stanley Works in 1948 and became executive vice president in 1962. He was president from 1966 to 1977 and chairman from 1977 to 1989.

Engineered for Growth

In 1962, Stanley executives took a chance on a brilliant inventor named Hugh L. Whitehouse, who wanted to create a new Stanley division that would sell air tools. Davis recalled that Whitehouse made a persuasive case that convinced the board of directors.

"He got an appointment with me and he came to my office one day. He had a briefcase, and in it he had some drawings of air tools. He convinced me that he knew what he was talking about. He said, 'I want to go into the air tool business and I need a backer and it would be a natural for Stanley. I liked this guy. I really believed in him. So I took his story to the board with my recommendation that we do it. I had him come into the meeting, and the board members liked him. So we embarked on the program. And basically, his plan worked. The tools not only worked, they were superior to what was on the market."[19]

The inside of a Stanley van, outfitted with the Uni-Rack display introduced in 1962. The van was a traveling showcase for the new display.

The division, established in Cleveland, Ohio, with Whitehouse as president and general manager, manufactured such products as drills, screwdrivers and grinders. The following year, the division added scaling hammers, nutsetters and impact wrenches to the line.[20]

In a continuing effort to consolidate functions, The Stanley Works in 1962 sold its Niles, Ohio, facility and transferred that site's responsibilities to the Hardware Division in New Britain.[21]

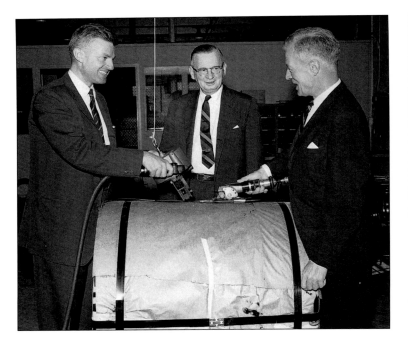

Above: In 1961, the Steel Strapping Division introduced a new line of air-powered tools for tensioning and sealing heavy-duty steel strapping. Assistant General Manager Donald W. Davis, left, demonstrates the two-ended sealer, while General Sales Manager James H.W. Conklin, right, demonstrates the tensioner. Between them stands Harrison Bristoll, general manager of the division. Wrapped and ready for shipment is a 5,200-pound coil of steel strapping.

Above right: The 1963 opening of Stanley's power tools plant was an important day in New Bern, North Carolina. Left to Right: Mack Lupton, mayor of New Bern; Leon J. Dunn, assistant general manager of Stanley's Power Tools Division; Terry Sandford, governor of North Carolina; Donald Davis, executive vice president of Stanley; and David Henderson, manager of the new plant.

Right: Stanley Tools moved this headquarters building on Myrtle Street in New Britain in 1964.

tor product lines, as well as Berry's manufacturing plant in Birmingham, Michigan.[29]

In 1966, The Stanley Works purchased Volkert Stampings, the Long Island manufacturer of stampings and components for major customers within the television, radio, spacecraft, and electronic equipment industries, as well as modular cabinets for industrial tool storage.[30] The name of the division was changed to Stanley-Vidmar in 1973.[31] Also in 1966, Stanley purchased a controlling interest in the Collins Company of Latin America, producer of machetes, axes, cane knives and shovels.[32]

As the *Hartford Courant* noted, The Stanley Works grew and prospered in the sixties.

"From 1962 through 1967, Stanley invested about $25 million in a new plant and equipment in the greater New Britain area. ... The company is now one of the 400 largest manufacturing corporations in the United States, with about 13,500 employees and 17,000 stockholders. About 50,000 different items are produced in Stanley plants, 30 of which are in the United States, eight in Canada and ten in eight other countries, including those in England, Germany, Italy, Mexico, Brazil, Colombia, Guatemala and Australia."[33]

As the company grew, it couldn't help but change character. John Parsons, a retired product line engineer, recalled the strong family feeling for which Stanley is known. Like many Stanley employees, *Parsons followed in the footsteps of his father, Stewart Parsons, who worked for the company 55 years, beginning in 1904. The combined service of the two men was more than 100 years. "We were a more cohesive group," John Parsons recalled. "We weren't down in North Carolina and Mexico and Taiwan and places like that. Everybody felt more like a family, closer together."[34]*

Right: The 1963 opening of Stanley's steel strapping facility in Pittsburg, California, was given a Stanley twist, with executives cutting a strip of steel instead of the traditional ribbon. Left to right: Bob Woodring, president of the Pittsburg Chamber of Commerce; Robert A. Langelier, Pittsburg plant manager; Bennett Lord, general manager of Stanley's Steel Strapping Division; Vernon Winsby, vice mayor of Pittsburg; and Donald W. Lasell, director of the Contra Costa Industrial Association.

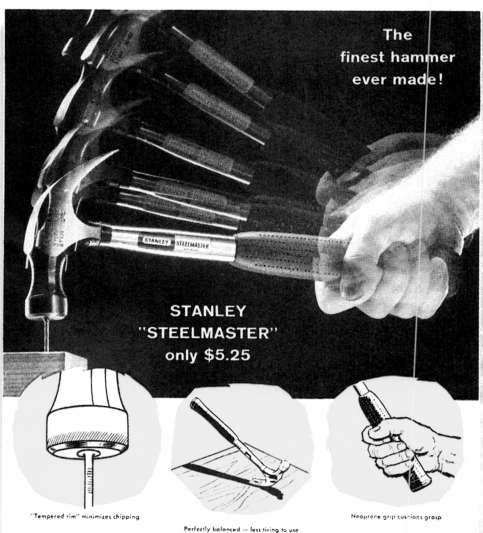

The
finest hammer
ever made!

STANLEY
"STEELMASTER"
only $5.25

"Tempered rim" minimizes chipping

Perfectly balanced -- less tiring to use

Neoprene grip cushions grasp

Heft it . . . swing it . . . smack it . . . this one has the right "feel" for work!

You instantly get the feel of balance and power when you pick up a Stanley *Steelmaster* hammer. And you like the cushioned, non-slip Neoprene grip. Now whack away with confidence -- the head is super heat-treated -- extra tough from face to claw, and the exclusive tempered rim minimizes chipping.

Your hardware dealer is now featuring Stanley hammers of every kind for every kind of work. But by all means try the finest

nail hammer ever made -- *Steelmaster*, a great hammer from Stanley.

HARDWARE
WEEK
SPECIAL

Stanley NAILMASTER Popular priced companion to the STEELMASTER hammer		
	Reg. Price --	$4.50
	NOW --	3.48
	YOU SAVE --	$1.02

Prices slightly higher in Canada

This 1960 advertisement reflected the company's growing emphasis on the Do-It-Yourself market.

CHAPTER TEN

DOING THINGS RIGHT

"We had a lot of industrial products, a lot of residential products and a lot of consumer products. I saw that we could put together quite a package of Do-It-Yourself products. And we could convert some products to Do-It-Yourself applications. If we could get kind of a theme for the company, and begin to build on that, it might do some great things for us."

— Donald W. Davis[1]

WHEN JOHN CAIRNS retired as chairman and president in 1966, after 42 years with The Stanley Works, the *Hartford Times* praised his many contributions to the company.

"Since 1950, when Cairns was elected president, Stanley sales have grown 2³/₄ times, from $60 million in 1949 to $165 million in 1965. Net worth has nearly doubled, increasing from $41,547,000 to $78,383,000. Stanley now employs more than 10,000 people in plants and offices around the globe."[2]

Donald W. Davis, at the age of 44, became the youngest person ever to serve as president of The Stanley Works. His enthusiasm, charisma, and community involvement brought new energy to the company. Davis was frequently profiled in newspapers and national trade publications. One article, printed about a year after Davis was elected, had the headline, "Don Davis — Young Head for an Old Company," and proclaimed, "Davis has brought new vigor and daring to Stanley's executive operations."[3] The article noted that Davis had brought a flair for marketing to The Stanley Works.

"Millions of consumers this fall undoubtedly witnessed a television commercial (probably on the Jackie Gleason Show or the Wide World of Sports or a Notre Dame football game) showing a Stanley Steelmaster hammer, cables attached, lifting a two-ton truck with a hippopotamus crammed inside. Or, if this dramatic demonstration failed to convince viewers that Stanley tools are incomparable for strength, quality, and power, a companion commercial showing a Stanley power drill rotating a carnival Ferris wheel with 12 happy kids giggling in the seats, may have been the clincher. 'This new use of TV,' Davis reports, 'is part of a planned program to increase even further the recognition and acceptance of the Stanley name and its famous "notched rectangle" trademark.'"[4]*

One of Davis' first actions as president was to list The Stanley Works on the New York Stock Exchange. Stanley had been selling its stock as a public company for nearly 100 years, but posting the stock on the "Big Board" was an important step for the company. Listed under the symbol

---

Above: The process of cold-rolling steel, pioneered by William Hart in 1870, was an important manufacturing method at The Stanley Works.

SWK on June 15, 1966, Stanley stock instantly became a popular recommendation of investors. *United States Investor* magazine was among the many publications touting the company.

"Although a relative newcomer to the New York Stock Exchange, Stanley, with its total of 14 divisions, 13 subsidiaries and three joint ventures, is one of the 400 largest industrial corporations in the United States. It is the leading full-line manufacturer of woodworking hand tools; the leader in builder's hardware; number one in cabinet hardware; and the third-ranking producer of steel strapping and strapping systems. Investors might also note that The Stanley Works has the 17th oldest record of continuous dividend payments of all companies on the Big Board. Stanley wrapped up one of the most eventful years in its 124-year history in 1966, with both sales and earnings rising to the highest levels ever attained by the company."[5]

By 1995, The Stanley Works could boast the longest continual period of both annual and

After 124 years in business, Stanley joined the New York Stock Exchange on June 15, 1966.

1966 – John Cairns retires and Donald Davis is elected president of The Stanley Works.

1968 – Davis creates the company slogan, "Stanley helps you do things right."

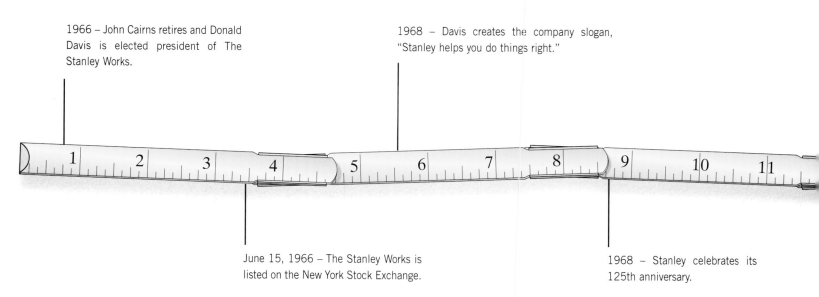

June 15, 1966 – The Stanley Works is listed on the New York Stock Exchange.

1968 – Stanley celebrates its 125th anniversary.

quarterly dividends of any industrial company on the New York Stock Exchange.[6]

Amerock

In late 1966, Stanley acquired the Amerock Corporation of Rockford, Illinois, an organization well-known for its decorative cabinet hardware.[7] A few years later, Stanley executives were shocked when the Federal Trade Commission forced The Stanley Works to divest its interest in the company. In 1974, after an antitrust ruling from the Federal Trade Commission, Stanley sold Amerock for $32 million.[8] In a recent interview, Davis described both the acquisition and the subsequent divestiture.

"We were very active in acquisitions at the time, and one acquisition that looked very attractive to us was Amerock Hardware. It was a family-owned business. The Aldeen family owned it. They loved their company, and they had built it from the ground up. It was a perfect fit. We were in the hardware business, but we weren't in cabinet hardware. An absolutely classic acquisition. We had an exchange of shares, and they became the largest Stanley shareholders.

"About two years after this happy event, I got a call from our general counsel, who said we had

Stanley Works President Donald W. Davis, center, watches Stanley stock during its first moments on the New York Stock Exchange.

gotten a call from the Federal Trade Commission. They were doing an investigation of the Amerock acquisition. My first reaction was, 'That's silly. Tell them we're not even in the same business and there couldn't possibly be any problem.' But it was serious.

"The rest of the story takes place over quite a few years. The trial examiner ruled against us,

1968 – The Sloane-Stanley Museum is created.

1974 – Stanley builds a new Corporate Laboratory.

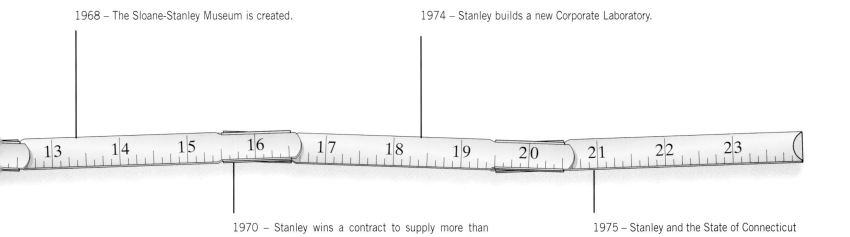

1970 – Stanley wins a contract to supply more than 100,000 architectural hinges for the World Trade Center in Manhattan.

1975 – Stanley and the State of Connecticut construct a fish ladder that helps migrating fish travel upstream.

and we appealed that with the Second Court of Appeals in New York. We had a split decision. Two upheld the trial examiner, one upheld The Stanley Works. The two that upheld the trial examiner did it on a different basis than he had ruled. He had ruled that it was a classic horizontal overlap. Amerock had 23 percent of the cabinet hardware market. Stanley had one half of 1 percent. Half of 1 percent in any other anti-trust case wasn't significant, but this guy said it was.

"The circuit court said the trial examiner was wrong. It wasn't illegal on the basis of horizontal overlap. But the court discovered it was illegal based on a theory called potential acquisition theory. This was considered an illegal acquisition because it reduced potential competition in that Stanley would be a logical entry into a cabinet hardware business, since they already make other kinds of hardware. If they buy Amerock, obviously they will not become a new competitor and therefore it is anti-competitive. Talk about a strange theory. We appealed to the Supreme Court, and it took another couple of years before they finally said they would not review it.

"So we were confronted with the task of divesting Amerock. It was the early seventies, and there was a deep recession. People weren't buying things, so we found no buyers for Amerock. If we didn't divest by a certain date, every day after that we would have to pay a huge fine of thousands of dollars per day. So

here we were in a recession with a very valuable, profitable company that we hated to lose.

"Here's where the really sad part starts. Up until now what I've told you is kind of a travesty of justice. But now the personal pressure comes into play. The Aldeens decide they love Stanley and they don't want to be sold to somebody else. So they wanted to buy back the business by giving us back part of the Stanley stock they had acquired.

"As the CEO of Stanley I had to get the best possible price for the shareholders. So my position was, 'Thank you very much for your offer but we've got to try to do a lot better.' We also, at that

Above: The Flaire shelving system, introduced in 1967, operated on a simple tension pole and bracket structure that was ideal for Do-It-Yourselfers.

Left: Amerock's headquarters in Rockford, Illinois. The promising acquisition turned sour for Stanley when the Federal Trade Commission claimed that it violated antitrust laws.

time, really wanted cash. Norris and Reuben Aldeen were still on our board and they had a total conflict of interest. In those days people were not as conscious of conflicts. I probably should have made a bigger issue of it. So here I am with my largest shareholders sitting on the board, wanting to buy the company back at a cut-rate price in a recession when nobody else wanted to buy it, with a fine of X thousands of dollars a day facing me for every day we missed the deadline.

"We finally got a company that showed some interest, Anchor Hocking. They made an offer that was basically book value and was cash. The board finally, reluctantly, agreed to the sale."[9]

The Do-It-Yourself Craze

In the late sixties, Davis wanted to find a unifying theme that would bring excitement and direction to the company. On a trip to the United Kingdom, he hit upon the idea of making Stanley the Do-It-Yourself Company.

"When I was in the Steel Strapping Division, I heard them talking about the DIY market. I thought that maybe we could hook our company to that star and this would become kind of an overarching focus for the company. We had a lot of industrial products, a lot of residential products and a lot of consumer products. I saw that we could put together quite a package of Do-It-Yourself products. And we could convert some products to Do-It-Yourself applications. If we could get a theme for the company, and begin to build on that, it might do some great things for us."[10]

Davis recalled that he personally thought up the company's slogan, "Stanley helps you do things right," in 1968.

"The agency was having trouble coming up with something. I was lying in bed one morning, thinking that it shouldn't be so difficult. It had

to be five or six words. It had to have the name Stanley in it. It had to be positive, and it had to cover everything we do and sell, so it had to be very general. If you're trying to do that in five or six words, it's not hard to come up with Stanley, customers, and what are they going to do with your products? It has to cover everything, from strapping a package with steel strapping or a sheet of metal, to using our tools. How do you do these things? First class. You do them right. Stanley, customers, you do all these things right. Stanley helps you do things right. It just flowed out.

"Now all I had to do was convince the agency. So I called the head of the agency and said, 'I know it's poor form for the client to come up with this, but I really think I have it and I don't want you to give me a snap reaction. I want you to have a meeting and talk about it. He called me back about two hours later, and said, 'We had our staff meeting. This is it. No question.'"[11]

A 1968 dinner in honor of Stanley's 125th anniversary. From left to right: U.S. Representative Thomas J. Meskill, Stanley President Donald Davis, U.S. Senator Abraham Ribicoff and New Britain Mayor Paul Manafort.

The company introduced several products in 1967 targeted for Do-It-Yourselfers, including Decor shelving and the Flaire line of adjustable shelves from the Hardware Division, and the Eager Beaver Circular saw, which cut forward or backward, left-handed or right-handed from the the Power Tools Division.[12]

In 1968, Hugh Whitehouse, president and general manager of the Air Tools Division, invented and patented an air shut-off control mechanism called a T valve. Today, the majority of torque control nutrunners on the market are equipped with this device.

The Sloane-Stanley Museum

The Stanley Works celebrated its 125th anniversary in 1968, commemorating the milestone with an anniversary dinner, family day and awards ceremony. The Stanley Works also commissioned a painting by Connecticut artist Steven Dohanos, which featured historical photographs and tools that symbolized Stanley's heritage. The Newcomen Society, a non-profit corporation that studies business, industrial and institutional history, honored Davis by inviting him to speak at one of its meetings.

Davis spearheaded the creation of the Sloane-Stanley Museum, a joint development between Davis and Eric Sloane, a Connecticut-based artist, writer, and collector of Americana. Sloane donated his extensive collection of antique tools to the State of Connecticut, and The Stanley Works donated 10 acres in Kent, Connecticut,

The company slogan, created by Davis in 1968.

Don Davis, center, donating 10 acres of land for the Sloane-Stanley Museum to Eric Hatch, chairman of the Connecticut Historical Commission. Left to right: artist Eric Sloane, whose collection is featured in the museum; Joseph Gill, state commissioner of agriculture; Davis; Hatch; and Howard Coe, Stanley's director of real estate.

and financed the construction of the museum. Governor John Dempsey announced that the donated land and the historic Kent Furnace would be known as a historical site.[13]

The 2,400-square-foot museum, which is still operated by the Connecticut Historical Commission, was dedicated on May 28, 1969.[14] Designed to replicate an early New England barn, the museum features a logging sled with spruce runners, corn mills, butter churns, apple butter pots, oyster rakes and a split rail fence. Tools on display include homemade broadaxes and adzes used by 17th century New England pioneers to build their cabins and barns, and the hatchets they borrowed or swiped from the Indians. One of the most interesting items is the 1805 diary of a farm boy, which served as inspiration for one of Sloane's books.[15]

The Strike of 1968

Labor difficulties at The Stanley Works were rare. Stanley Works employees generally stayed for decades, and inspired other family members to join the company as well. In 1956, for example, 19 employees celebrated 50 years of employment at The Stanley Works. They were given miniature Stanley Tool Boxes filled with silver hardware and 50 silver dollars. The same year, the company announced that 744 employees had been given watches to celebrate 25 years with the company.[16]

But in 1968, labor relations at The Stanley Works suffered a strain when a strike impaired operations at all seven New Britain divisions. Richard C. Hastings, who was president and general manager of the Stanley Tools Division at the time, recalled that the strike was difficult for everybody involved. "I felt that the company and the union just weren't communicating," he said.

"The company and the employees just couldn't figure out how to save face. It was such a terrible waste of time. The union was being paid in full for time spent negotiating. I wouldn't want to do that again for anything. But from another viewpoint, it was time well-spent, because we established ground rules on how we were going to operate."[17]

The strike lasted four months, ending in mid-May when employees were awarded two-year

The exterior of the Sloane-Stanley Museum, designed to replicate an early New England barn.

contracts that allowed The Stanley Works to remain competitive, while providing wages and benefits that were comparable with other progressive companies.

The Kidnapping

Another dramatic event took place in 1968 when two company executives were kidnapped by a criminal posing as an Internal Revenue Service agent. As the *Hartford Times* reported, the executives escaped without injury.

"After arriving, the 'dapper bandit' exposed a .38-caliber revolver and opened an attaché case and let the two executives view five sticks of dynamite which were wired to a battery and a ring on the outside of the case. Inside the case was a small pistol — possibly a Beretta. The gunman told the executives that he would destroy himself and anyone near him should he fail to get his way. After detailing his plans to the officials, the gunman ordered Edwards to telephone the New Britain Bank & Trust Company and make arrangements for the withdrawal of $34,000 in $10 and $20 denominations. ... The money

The 1970 groundbreaking for a new air tools plant in Mayfield Village, Ohio. Pictured from left to right: Hoyt Pease, vice president of manufacturing; Vincent Busa, mayor of Mayfield Village; Joseph H. Myers, group vice president of Stanley Industrial Divisions; and Albert F. Clear, executive vice president of The Stanley Works. Hugh L. Whitehouse, general manager of the Stanley Air Tools Division, is operating the bulldozer.

passed hands about 4:30 p.m. The gunman, who stutters when under tension, acted coolly as he paraded the men to Freedell's automobile. He ordered Freedell to drive to the Scott Swamp Game Sanctuary in Farmington — more than five miles from the plant. There, the gunman forced the two men into the trunk of the car. The two executives were able to work their way free with a pair of pliers they found in the trunk."[18]

The Seventies

Stanley opened the decade with new products, acquisitions, and manufacturing plants. The Astro 3 install-it-yourself automatic garage door opener, the Stanley Guardware line of security hardware, and the Carriage House Collection of cabinet hard-

ware were among the products introduced in 1970. New tools included a line of heavy-duty production routers, a pocket-size hacksaw, a flower shear with a replaceable Slimknife blade, and a 20-foot Powerlock rule. Stanley also acquired a contract in 1970 to supply more than 100,000 architectural hinges for the construction of the World Trade Center in Manhattan.[19]

Thanks in part to the company's new emphasis on Do-It-Yourself items, the Stanley Works overcame a sluggish economy in 1970 to establish record sales of $257.6 million for the year, realizing net earnings of $12.4 million. Davis gave credit for this achievement to the company's employees, noting in the 1970 Annual Report that, "Stanley's good performance in 1970 can be credited to the good performance of people — the 13,500 employees who make up The Stanley Works."[20]

In 1971, Donald Davis was one of two recipients of the McAuliffe Medal, an award "conferred annually on a representative of management and labor who has introduced into industrial relations in Connecticut a spirit of goodwill and cooperation."[21] It was one of a great many honors that would be conferred upon Davis during his years at Stanley, in tribute to his leadership abilities and community service.

International and Domestic Expansion

In 1970, Stanley purchased the assets of S.A. Wetty & Sons, Inc. of Royersford, Pennsylvania, a company that manufactured extruded and molded plastic parts. Expansion of existing facilities included a new air tools plant in Mayfield Village, Ohio, an addition to the hammer manufacturing facility at the Atha plant in New Jersey, and expansion of the Eagle Square plant in South Shaftsbury, Vermont.[22]

The company also continued its international expansion in 1970, acquiring the firm of Walter Finkeldei, GmbH, of Wuppertal, Germany, manufacturer of spiral ratchet screwdrivers, power bits and socket and ratchet wrenches. Stanley also acquired a controlling interest in S.A. Quenot-Mabo, Besançon, France, a company that manufactured linear measuring instruments. Stanley-Titan of Australia expanded its line by purchasing the outstanding shares of Turner Industries, Ltd., an Australian manufacturer of hacksaws, bandsaws and other tools.[23]

In 1971, growth continued with the acquisitions of Bumeda Steel Productions, Ltd. of Montreal, Canada; Prestressed Concrete of Colorado, Inc.; and the Ackley Manufacturing Company of Portland, Oregon, a manufacturer of hydraulic tools.[24] The Stanley Works also purchased Stanley-Brockhaus, manufacturer of steel strapping in Gelsenkirchen-Buer, Germany. The company was renamed Stanley Packsystem GmbH, but was sold in 1975.[25] In 1972, Stanley built a new manufacturing facility for Stanley Works Italia, south of Rome.[26]

Acquisitions in 1973 included Antichoc, S.A., manufacturer of levels in Saint-Louis, France; William Mills, Ltd., producer of garden tools in Sheffield, England; and the Pennsylvania Saw Corporation, of York, Pennsylvania.[27]

The results of the vigorous expansion policy were realized in the form of increased revenue, and in 1973, sales jumped 23 percent over the previous year.[28] In the 1973 Annual Report, Davis attributed the growth to an increase in the Do-It-Yourself market, along with a growing list of acquisitions.

The Stanley Works built a new Corporate Laboratory in 1974, and equipped it with state-of-the-art technology. One of the more unusual features was the lack of a front door. The building's main entrance was "separated from the elements, not by a door but only by a curtain of warm air.

Stanley's Corporate Laboratory, built in 1974.

An aerial view of the Rainbow Dam, where The Stanley Works constructed a ladder to help migrating fish swim upstream.

A creation of the company's Door Operating Equipment Division in Farmington, the curtain features a controlled, downward flow of air that makes standard doors unnecessary."[29] The energy crisis of the seventies later prompted the company to reconsider its use of heat, and Stanley installed doors in the laboratory.

Though a deep economic crisis gripped the nation during the middle of the decade, Stanley sales remained solid. In 1974, sales were $487 million, and the following year, they dropped only 5 percent to $464 million.[30]

The Stanley Works was becoming a global, sophisticated company, recalled Richard Huck, chief financial officer since 1993. Huck began working in the general accounting office of The Stanley Works in 1970 and became a corporate officer in 1990, when he was made vice president and con-

Thanks to the fish ladder, constructed in 1975, salmon are now able to migrate upstream through the Rainbow Dam.

troller.[31] Like many Stanley Works employees, Huck grew up in New Britain. "As a youngster, I thought of Stanley as a lot of big factory buildings," he said. "But from the inside, I learned that there was a lot more sophistication inside the company than was apparent from the bricks on the outside."[32] The company's financial system in 1975 was one of the most advanced in the country, he said.

"I can recall one instance where I went to a cash-management seminar down in New Orleans. ... I remember Mobil Oil and a number of other oil companies were there, some strong, capable companies. I remember coming away from that saying, 'You know, there were some pretty reputable companies, but when it came down to the systems that we had in place and the activities that we used in mobilizing our cash, at least in the United States, we were pretty sophisticated.' That was a good feeling.

"The cash-management system that was in place 20 years ago is, for the most part, still there today. It's a sophisticated system for moving cash among business units with a minimal amount of cash coming from any one place. It operates on what's called a zero-balance system, where all the operating units zero out the balance every day, and concentrate the cash in one place, where it has visibility and where you can manage it in terms of investment."[33]

The Rainbow Fish Ladder

In an impressive example of public-private partnership, The Stanley Works teamed up with state and federal officials to create a ladder that helped migrating salmon swim up the Farmington River. The salmon had been blocked by the Rainbow Dam, constructed by The Stanley Works in 1924 to provide power for company facilities.

In 1975, after it had been determined that the dam was an obstacle to salmon, Davis spearheaded an innovative project that solved the problem. Stanley Works engineers, working with state and federal officials, created a fish ladder around the dam. Stanley shared the $750,000 cost for the project with the State of Connecticut.[34]

Field & Stream magazine praised The Stanley Works for the partnership effort.

"The ladder is designed to provide a way for 20,000 American shad and hopefully 5,000 Atlantic salmon to ascend by their own locomotion a total of 59 feet, the height of the dam. It also features fish traps, viewing rooms, and automatic cameras, all the equipment needed to monitor and control the flow of the fish. The Rainbow Dam is, of course, still functional as a hydroelectric plant. ... The Farmington River is destined to become a renowned example of what can happen when the relationship between industry and the environment is made compatible."[35]

The ladder was a success, and many salmon benefited from it. That year, The Stanley Works was awarded the New Samaritan Citation for Excellence, for "activities responsive to human needs and excellence in community involvement." The Rainbow Fish Ladder played a major role in the choice of The Stanley Works for the award, but the New Samaritan Corporation also honored The Stanley Works for "minority employment, craftsmanship, ecology, and other areas."[36]

In a tribute to the company's community service and overall excellence, The Stanley Works won the prestigious American Eagle Award in 1980.

CHAPTER ELEVEN

CORPORATE CITIZENSHIP & EXHILARATING GROWTH

"We are particularly active in the area of affordable housing. We support sweat-equity projects like Habitat for Humanity with sound professional advice and donations of the best tools and home improvement products in the world."

— 1993 Annual Report.[1]

IN 1976, THE STANLEY Works donated 159 acres to the State of Connecticut and The Nature Conservancy, so that it would be preserved and protected forever. The land, situated along the Housatonic River in Kent, Connecticut, includes the picturesque St. Johns Ledges, a mile-long rock formation, 600 feet high, overlooking the river. Another parcel increased the property of the Sloane-Stanley Museum by 15 acres.

The gifts were formally received in a ceremony at the museum attended by Governor Ella Grasso, who praised the generosity of The Stanley Works. "On behalf of all citizens of our state, it is a pleasure to thank The Stanley Works for this generous donation of land to the people of Connecticut," she said.[2]

The tradition of public service at The Stanley Works began with founder Frederick T. Stanley, who served as both warden and mayor of New Britain, and was instrumental in bringing running water and railroad service to the community. Since that time, the company has contributed resources and volunteer hours to a wide variety of causes.

In 1970, Donald Davis formalized the tradition by creating a Public Policy Council of 20 employees from various Stanley Works locations. The panel members make decisions based on the recommendations of five sub-committees, which include Health and Human Services, Housing and Neighborhoods, Arts and Culture, Education, and General Contributions. According to Davis, the sub-committees are the core of the program.

"Members represent a cross-section of Stanley employees, with each chairman serving on the council. In this way, we maximize employee involvement yet remain a reasonably sized group. They research requests, help define community needs, initiate projects, and ultimately develop solutions that could involve Stanley volunteer support, challenge grants, matching gifts, or just about anything needed to get the job done."[3]

Based on the recommendations of the sub-committees, the panel approved a $1,500 scholarship for a student majoring in metallurgy at the University of Connecticut in 1977.[4] Later that year, an easement was granted to the United

Above: Stanley is proud to support Habitat for Humanity, the grassroots organization that helps build homes for American families.

Employees of The Stanley Works volunteered for this all-woman Habitat for Humanity project in Charlotte, North Carolina, in 1991. Back row, left to right: Susan Hancock of Habitat for Humanity, Rosalynn Carter, Angela Harris of The Stanley Works and Donna Alexander of The Stanley Works. In the front row, all from The Stanley Works: Judy Esposito, Brenda March and Cheryl Farmer.

1976 — Stanley donates 159 acres of land to the State of Connecticut and The Nature Conservancy.

1980 — Stanley adds facilities in Michigan, Vermont, Connecticut and Ohio.

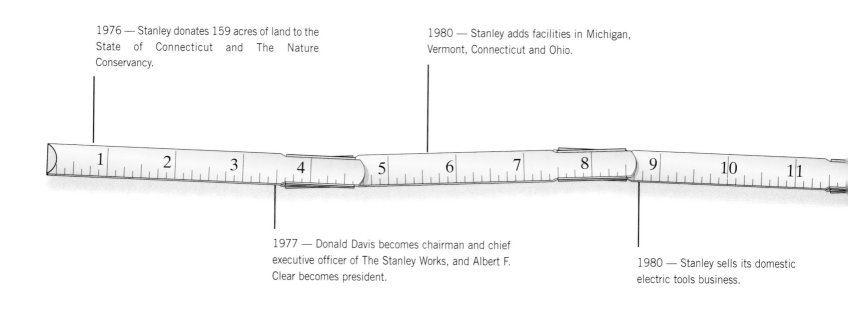

1977 — Donald Davis becomes chairman and chief executive officer of The Stanley Works, and Albert F. Clear becomes president.

1980 — Stanley sells its domestic electric tools business.

States Forest Service, giving perpetual access to four miles of the Appalachian Trail and the Long Trail in Vermont.[5]

In 1979, actions included a $4,000 grant to Junior Achievement of North Central Connecticut; a $1,200 donation to the Linfield, Connecticut, Volunteer Fire Company, and a $500 grant to the Independent College Fund, as requested by the Stanley Power Tools Division in New Bern.[6]

By 1995, direct contributions had reached $1.6 million a year, said Patricia McLean, manager of corporate communications.[7] The company has an extensive matching gifts program, in which it gives a dollar for every dollar an employ-

Above, right: Stanley Works CEO Richard Ayers confers with Rosalynn Carter during a 1991 Habitat for Humanity project in Miami.

Right: Former President Jimmy Carter and a future homeowner take a break during a Habitat for Humanity home-building project. As supporters of the grass roots organization, The Carters hammer and paint alongside other Habitat volunteers.

1980 — Stanley acquires Mac Tools.

1980 — Stanley wins the American Eagle Award from The American Supply & Machinery Manufacturers' Association, Inc.

1980 — Stanley acquires Compo-Cast.

ee contributes to a qualified college or university. Matching funds are also available for donations to public television or radio, emergency services, soup kitchens, food banks, shelters, and education for kindergarten through 12th grade.

The Stanley Works is especially active in building-related activities, such as Habitat for Humanity, the grass roots organization that builds homes for American families. The organization, long a favorite of former President Jimmy Carter, uses volunteer labor and tax-deductible donations to build and renovate housing for Americans who lack decent shelter. Stanley contributes tools, funds and publicity to the cause, and employees contribute many volunteer hours.

"We are particularly active in the area of affordable housing," noted the 1993 Annual Report. "We support sweat-equity projects like Habitat for Humanity with sound professional advice and donations of the best tools and home improvement products in the world. Our broad line of entry doors, closet doors, mirrors and closet organizers are particularly welcome contributions for new homeowners."[8]

Another popular cause is disaster relief. In 1982, volunteers from The Stanley Works helped the American Red Cross after unusually heavy rains flooded parts of Connecticut.[9] In 1983, the company donated $1,500 and several kits of Stanley tools to help residents of southeastern Australia rebuild after severe brush fires.[10] When an earthquake measuring 8.1 on the Richter scale struck Mexico City in 1985, The Stanley Works responded with $5,000 for the purchase of medical supplies, bedding and blankets for the injured and homeless.[11] Similar efforts were made after Hurricane Gilbert struck the Caribbean in 1988 and Hurricane Andrew struck South Florida and Louisiana in 1992.

Over the years, organizations that have been helped by The Stanley Works have included the New Britain YMCA, the Leukemia Society of America, and the Ad Council, which provides powerful public service messages. The Stanley

During the 1987 Connecticut Special Olympics sports event for handicapped athletes, 25 Stanley Works employees, family members and friends served as assistant coaches for Special Olympians from New Britain.

Works is also active in the Special Olympics, the United Way, the March of Dimes, the American Red Cross, and the Big Brother/Big Sister Program.

Above: The Stanley Works supported the Build-A-Dream program in 1986. Working with local volunteers, the program donates cash, tools and volunteer incentives to help build playgrounds such as this one at the DiLoreto School in New Britain, Connecticut.

Exhilarating Growth

One reason The Stanley Works has been able to give generously of its resources is that the company has been financially successful. In 1976, The Stanley Works emerged from the mid-seventies recession with sales of $566.3 million, a remarkable 21 percent increase over the previous year. New products introduced that year included the Top-Reading Powerlock rule, a woodchopper's maul, and a line of plastic mallets intended for Do-It-Yourselfers.[12] The company also took complete ownership of its Australian operation by acquiring Titan's half of the business.

In 1977, Donald Davis, at the age of 55, vacated the presidency to become chairman and chief executive officer of The Stanley Works, a post that had remained vacant the previous 10 years. Davis had a strong sense of the importance of social responsibility on the part of The Stanley Works and its employees. In 1977, he was selected to be chairman of the Connecticut Business and Industry Association (CBIA), the state's largest business group.[13] CBIA President Arthur L.

Below: CEO Richard Ayers chats with other Stanley volunteers during a March of Dimes WalkAmerica fundraiser.

Woods commented that, "Mr. Davis exemplifies the quality of business leadership we have in Connecticut and its energetic dedication to the creation of jobs and a vigorous economy."[14]

Albert F. Clear was elected to succeed Davis as president. Clear had been with The Stanley Works since 1965, serving as executive vice president since 1969.

In the second half of the seventies, the company's focus on the growing Do-It-Yourself market paid off handsomely. Sales increased a dramatic 20 percent in 1977, reaching $640.2 million. To tap into the growing market, Stanley introduced such products as a plastic marking gauge, a versatile cutting tool called a Handyshear, and an assortment of new levels, screwdrivers, squares, metric nut drivers and measuring tapes.

Sales for 1978 rose 28 percent over the previous year, reaching $753.8 million, and new products included a line of consumer and professional router bits, a line of Leverlock tape rules, an economy wire stripper, and a sawbuck bracket made especially for homeowners who cut their own firewood.[15]

Above: Richard Ayers (front row, right) poses with members of the Home Builders Institute at the annual convention of the National Association of Home Builders in January 1992.

Left: Senator Paul Simon and Richard Ayers display the "Hands that Work" award from the Home Builders Institute during the annual convention of the National Association of Home Builders in 1992.

The following year saw another huge boost in sales, which climbed an astounding 24 percent to $872.3 million.[16] The record results were credited to the continuing Do-It-Yourself craze, as *Business Week* noted.

"During the 1974-75 recession, Do-It-Yourself sales actually advanced 27 percent, and the industry's growth has been about 17 percent annually since then. Moreover, Stanley's strategic move toward this market is prompting a radical transformation of the company. Today, this once-stodgy metalwork manufacturer is looking more and more like an aggressive consumer product marketer. Stanley, the nation's leading producer of hand tools, now garners roughly 50 percent of its business from sales to Do-It-Yourselfers. Davis hopes to lift that figure to 60 percent soon."[17]

Below: Organizers were overwhelmed by donations to a November 1989 Care & Share food drive sponsored by The Stanley Works. Standing, from left to right: Mark Nalawajek, Angie Levesque, Joanne Machado, Rev. David Mellon, Bessie Boyd, Alan Martin, Juan Rivera, Bernadette Schuster and Reno Levesque. Kneeling, from left to right: Cheryl Farmer and George Griffin.

To focus more exclusively on the successful Do-It-Yourself market, The Stanley Works decided to discontinue its garden tool line in 1977, after years of competing unsuccessfully against larger, more well-established garden tool rivals. A *Business Week* article explained the decision. "In any given line, Davis wants the company to be number one or close to it. 'We want to have a leadership role, we don't want to be number four, five or six,' he explained."[18]

Above: When Stanley advertised its DIY doll-house on television in the late seventies, it received thousands of requests for the product.

Right: The back cover of the detailed plan book, showing the finished dollhouse.

An Aggressive Marketing Strategy

The Do-It-Yourself market was growing at a remarkable pace, and Stanley was the leading Do-It-Yourself company. According to Stanley's 1977 Annual Report, the industry was six times bigger than boating, and eight times bigger than fishing, hunting and camping combined.[19] To illustrate

the dominance of the market, the company aired a television commercial showing a hammer smashing a tennis ball, with the announcement that the Do-It-Yourself market was 27 times bigger than tennis.[20]   Davis promoted The Stanley Works aggressively, increasing the advertising budget by 73 percent between 1976 and 1979.[21]

The growth was not limited to the United States, noted the 1978 Annual Report. "Sales of DIY products in Europe registered good progress. Latin America, which was previously not a factor in the DIY market, began to experience substantial growth in this area in 1978."[22]

By 1979, two-thirds of all Americans were undertaking Do-It-Yourself projects, and more money was spent by Do-It-Yourselfers than by professional builders. Stanley dominated this $22.1 billion market.[23] As Davis explained to one newspaper reporter:

> *"I really see this as not a trend or a movement or a fad. I see it as a very pervasive, permanent part of our society. For the foreseeable future, people are going to be doing this kind of thing, where 10 or 20 years ago they did not."[24]*

The Stanley Works ended the decade with record sales and earnings, and, more importantly, with a reputation as the biggest name in the country's favorite weekend hobby. To continue improving the company's profits and image, Davis established several programs to help Do-It-Yourselfers use Stanley products, as he explained to a newspaper reporter in 1979.

> *"[Stanley] sometimes sets up film strips in retail outlets to illustrate particular projects, and it provides a toll-free number with its garage door opener so technicians can guide customers through an installation if they have trouble. We*

try to design a product that will be easy to use. We try to tell him how to use it. We package it in such a way that he can see exactly what the product is and what its purpose is,' Davis said.

"'If a Do-It-Yourselfer buys something, takes it home and has a lot of trouble with it, it's going to turn him off. We're in this for the long pull. We want to start from the ground up — right from the design of the product, the packaging of the merchandise, the instructions, the display and the follow-up.'

"'As an illustration, company advertising asks people who buy the garage door openers to fill out a card. Sometimes their suggestions are incorporated into revised instructions. Everything is thought through as to how to make this a successful venture for the Do-It-Yourselfer. So when he's through with a project, he has a positive feel-

ing toward our company and our product. That's the whole thrust of our television commercials. You get some satisfaction from working with your hands, doing your own thing.'"[25]

A new retail environment accompanied the stunning growth in the Do-It-Yourself market.

"Big hardware stores, home centers, lumber and building supply stores — these are the scenes for free clinics that show consumers how to build, how to paint, how to remodel, how to conserve energy. One can find almost everything needed to build a house, from basement to rooftop, in most of the one-stop-shopping home centers. There are 7,500 of them today. Ten years ago they didn't exist."[26]

By 1980, an estimated $30.9 billion was spent on Do-It-Yourself products in the United States.[27] Even a nationwide economic downturn in 1980 did not stop Stanley's progress, though the

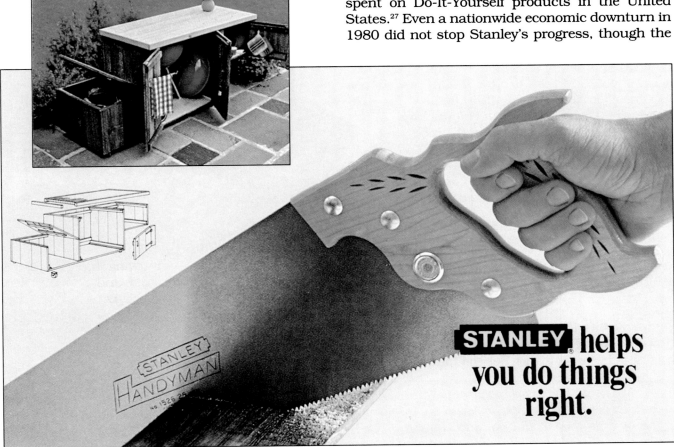

STANLEY helps you do things right.

A 1975 advertisement for Stanley saws and free barbecue plans. Above, a completed barbecue project.

Mac Tools

Above: Mechanics gather around the Mac tools van, placing orders and discussing new products.

In 1980, The Stanley Works made two important acquisitions — Mac Tools and Compo-Cast. Mac Tools, of Ohio, produced a top-quality line of auto-repair tools that it sold directly from vans to mechanics across the United States and Canada. Compo-Cast manufactured a unique line of "dead blow" striking tools that were exceptionally easy to use.[37]

Below: Mac Tools sponsored racer Ernie Irvan in the Busch Grand National in 1991.

Mac Tools sells a traditional line of sockets, wrenches, screw-drivers, and similar prod-ucts, 40 percent of which are manufactured in facto-ries in Dallas and Wichita Falls, Texas. The division keeps a high profile in the world of auto racing, and sponsors many of the nation's top racers, including Jeff Gordon, Ernie Irvan, Ricky Rudd, Mark Martin and Dale Jarrett. "The asso-ciation that Mac has enjoyed with racing is without question our biggest brand-builder," said Charles Blossom, president of the division since 1992.[38]

Blossom praised The Stanley Works for allowing Mac to keep an individual identity within the Stanley family. "Mac has been in business some 53 or 54 years now," he said. "I think that The Stanley Works, and correctly so, recognized that the Mac brand name was a significant piece of the equity that it had purchased, and it wanted to maintain that high-quality and unique image. They have really done a pretty good job of that."[39]

CEO Ayers recalled that Mac was "literally on the edge of bankruptcy" when Stanley acquired it in 1980. As the company's established trouble-shooter, Ayers was given the task of reviving the company. "It was a lot of fun because it was a business that was just crying out for leadership," he recalled.

"The first thing they needed was money. There were some very difficult things that had happened to them over the prior couple of years that had split the organization. They had lost a number of their distributors and they just flat ran out of money. They were not meeting payroll. They were not able to buy the materials to keep their operations running. So the first thing they needed was an infusion of cash.

"They also needed some people at the top who were willing to listen to what the field organization was reporting needed to be done in terms of product additions, finance programs, and in terms of just supporting the dealer network."[40]

Across-the-Board Quality

In 1980, The Stanley Works was presented with the American Eagle Award in recognition of "its unusual across-the-board quality."[41] Factors that helped Stanley win the annual award from The American Supply & Machinery Manufacturers' Association, Inc., were its 20-employee Public Affairs Advisory Committee, which sought out opportunities for community service; its participation in the construction of the Rainbow fish ladder; and its donation of land to The Nature Conservancy and the State of Connecticut.[42]

Davis was chosen by *Time* magazine in 1981 to accompany 16 editors and 31 of the nation's top businessmen on a 17,000-mile tour of nine European and Persian Gulf nations.[43] The group interviewed Lech Walesa in Paris and went on to visit Poland, Moscow, Hungary, Yugoslavia, Saudi Arabia, Kuwait, Oman and Egypt. According to *Time*, the purpose of the trip was to give the participants an opportunity "to explore for yourselves some of the intricate political, economic and sociological conditions in those parts of the world."[44] The *New Britain Herald* recorded Davis' impression of the journey.

"After the exhausting tour, Davis said he came home convinced that 'the concept of a controlled, repressive society is breaking down. Communism is a bankrupt system.' ... Davis said he believed the group, because it included so many top U.S. business leaders, plus Time *editors, was able to open doors that neither the editors nor the businessmen could otherwise expect to crack alone."*[45]

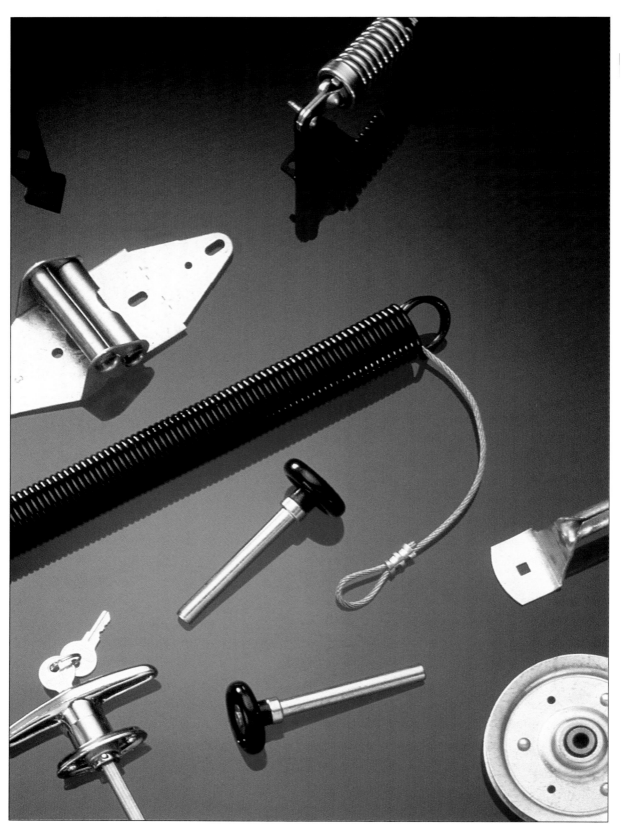

Throughout its long history, The Stanley Works has remained loyal to both its original product of hardware and its original community of New Britain, Connecticut. Shown here are some of the garage door hardware products sold by The Stanley Works.

CHAPTER TWELVE

HARDWARE CITY OF THE WORLD

"It was a step toward amending the city's marred public image, a chance to rekindle economic interest there."

— The *Hartford Courant*, 1981,
on Stanley's plans to build its World Headquarters in New Britain[1]

IN 1981, Vaughn E. West was elected president and chief operating officer of The Stanley Works. West had been hired in 1971 as corporate controller, and was later promoted to vice president for finance. Albert Clear was given the new title of vice chairman of corporate development.[2]

Donald Davis, chairman from 1977 to 1989, appreciated West's skills in finance and computers, but conceded he had some doubts about West as president.[3] As it turned out, West was president of The Stanley Works for only a short period of time. After he left, Arthur E. Gledhill, a 28-year veteran of The Stanley Works, became the next president.

A Painful Cutback

After the incredible success of the late seventies and early eighties, The Stanley Works experienced a shock in 1982, when earnings fell a dramatic 32 percent from the previous year, impaired by depressed economic activity throughout the world.[4] The Stanley Works was forced to cut back in many areas, including a painful, but necessary, 18 percent reduction in staff.[5]

R. Alan Hunter, who was then controller of the Hand Tools Division and is today president and chief operating officer, said several factors contributed to the company's financial difficulties.

"Mortgage rates were 17 and 18 percent, and the construction industry virtually collapsed. That was the short-term issue. The longer-term issue was this new thing called foreign imports. The competition from imports had traditionally been competition from Japanese manufacturers, which was tough competition, but it was okay. The new competition that was beginning to take place was very low-cost competition, which fortunately, in many instances, was also low-quality. But a lot of the retail folks felt they really needed to look at it. It was very threatening to the organization."[6]

The setback was an awakening for the company, and dramatic steps were needed to reverse the situation. To fight foreign competition, particularly from Taiwan, The Stanley Works came up with a marketing approach known as the plain white vanilla program, as Davis explained.

The Stanley Works acquired Proto Industrial Tools, manufacturer of sockets, wrenches and other products, in 1984.

Arthur E. Gledhill was president of The Stanley Works from 1982 to 1985.

"Our bread-and-butter tools, like tapes and screwdrivers, were high-volume items. Our customers could buy them from competitors for 40 percent less than our items. The quality wasn't as good, but it was acceptable. All the large retail outlets and chains were telling us, 'We love Stanley. We love your products. They are the highest quality, and we'll pay 10, 12 or maybe 15 percent extra for that. But we can't pay 40 percent.'

"We couldn't let these markets go, because it would be too hard to win them back. So we came up with something that we called the plain white vanilla program. We said, 'We're going to take all these high-volume items that the Taiwanese are selling and get within 10 to 15 percent of their price. We're going to make customers compare apples to apples.'

"Now, they're buying this stuff from Taiwan and they think they're getting this huge bargain. The fact of the matter is, we're providing a tremendous number of services that the Taiwanese are not providing. We listed 32 of these things, including volume discounts, advertising co-op money, merchandising support, quick delivery of small quantities, etc.

"We went to these large customers and said, 'We have a plain white vanilla program to com-

1981 — Albert Clear is named vice chairman of corporate development, and Vaughn E. West becomes president and chief operating officer of The Stanley Works.

1983 — The Taylor Rental Corporation is acquired.

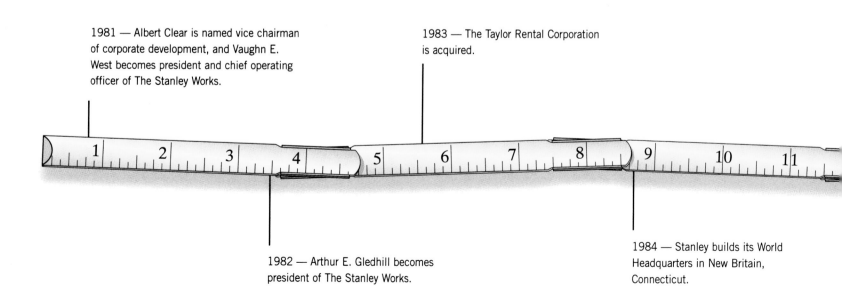

1982 — Arthur E. Gledhill becomes president of The Stanley Works.

1984 — Stanley builds its World Headquarters in New Britain, Connecticut.

pete with the Taiwanese or anybody else. The price schedule is within 10 percent to 15 percent of their prices, but you have to order it three months in advance, and there won't be any merchandise help, advertising allowance, or volume discount.' Some looked at it and said, 'Okay, we'll do it.' Others said, 'We'll keep what you have.' But we stopped the deterioration of the market."[7]

The Stanley Works continued to focus on the successful Do-It-Yourself market, introducing Workmaster sockets and wrenches for DIY auto repair, and the Stan-Guard garage door opener and security system for DIY installation, which guarded against intrusion, smoke and carbon monoxide. An advertising program called The Great Stanley Rebate brought a strong response from consumers who received rebates from tags on specially-packaged tools. The Weather Station line of energy-conservation products was also successful.[8]

Chairman Donald Davis, standing, and President Arthur E. Gledhill, seated, in a 1982 photograph.

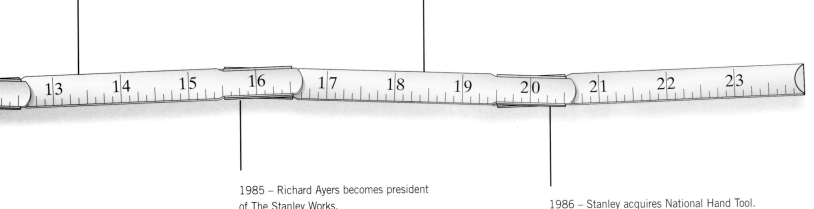

1984 – Stanley acquires Proto Industrial Tools from Ingersoll-Rand.

1986 – The Bostitch fastener and fastening tool business is purchased from Textron Inc.

1985 – Richard Ayers becomes president of The Stanley Works.

1986 – Stanley acquires National Hand Tool.

Richard Hastings retired in 1983, and Richard H. Ayers, who had been with Stanley 11 years, succeeded him as group vice president of the Hand Tools Group.[9]

Taylor Rental

The plain white vanilla program, along with other initiatives and a general improvement in the economy, helped The Stanley Works get back on track. Business picked up again in 1983, and earnings rose an astonishing 41 percent from the previous year.[10] One of the year's most important acquisitions was Taylor Rental Corporation, a tool rental company with 560 franchised rental centers in 49 states. The company rented high-ticket items, such as pressure cleaners or wet saws, to light contractors and Do-It-Yourselfers.

Stanley garage door openers were as easy to transport as they were to install. Sold in a single carton that could fit easily in the trunk of a car, it came complete with installation hardware and easy-to-follow illustrated instructions.

Shortly after the acquisition, Davis explained why Taylor was a welcome addition to The Stanley Works.

"Worldwide competition has become more intense as world markets shrink and cut across countries with more and more ease. Because manufactured products can be produced at lower and lower costs around the world, one of our strategies is to become less dependent upon basic manufacturing and to expand into more service industries. That approach will give Stanley a uniqueness that is less vulnerable to lower production costs in other parts of the world. That trend will not result in any drastic changes, just a move to better capitalize on our strength in the Do-It-Yourself market, where the Stanley name is known around the world."[11]

The Hardware City of the World

In 1984, The Stanley Works built its World Headquarters in New Britain, making The Stanley Works the only hardware company still based in the New England city. New Britain, once known as the Hardware City of the World, could once again proudly claim the title. According to the *Hartford Courant,* "It was a step toward amending the city's marred public image, a chance to rekindle economic interest there."[12]

While other hardware companies had either gone out of business or moved away, The Stanley Works continued to grow and prosper in the city where it had been founded 141 years earlier. Ronald Gilrain, retired vice president of public affairs and marketing, noted that The Stanley Works has shown incredible loyalty toward the community and the people who helped build it into a great institution.

The Stanley Works has been a positive force in New Britain in ways that go beyond its capacity as the city's major employer. The company contributes generously to local schools, libraries, and other organizations. In addition, it takes an active role in improving opportunities for New Britain residents, said Gilrain.

"At one time, New Britain had people flooding in from Eastern Europe — Russia, Poland,

As part of an ongoing effort to capture the growing Do-It-Yourself market, Stanley introduced the U-install line of products, which included this easy-to-install door.

lot of people who need the kind of jobs that are no longer available.

"Our efforts have been to work with the schools and the people of New Britain on programs that benefit and help retain existing employees. We want to provide better educational support and direction for young people so they don't fall out of the system. We at Stanley have been very active in educational programs."[13]

The Stanley Works moved into the new 104,000-square-foot headquarters in August 1984. In recognition of his ongoing efforts to improve New Britain, Davis was named "New Britain Man of the Year" in 1984 by the New Britain Elks and other community leaders. At the time, Davis was not only chairman and chief executive officer of The Stanley Works, but he was also the incoming president of United Community Services, honorary cam-

the Ukraine — to work in the factories of Stanley and half a dozen other companies that are no longer in business. But the world has changed, and Stanley no longer has those kinds of entry-level jobs. With few exceptions, Stanley is looking for people with good numeric skills, good linguistic skills, and now, people with computer skills, who are able to contribute to the manufacturing process. That has meant that we are in a community where there are a

Proto Industrial Tools, acquired by Stanley in 1984, manufactures a wide variety of heavy-duty industrial tools.

Proto Tools

In 1984, Stanley purchased Proto Industrial Tools from Ingersoll-Rand, and the Stanley-Proto Industrial Tools Division was created.[16] "We are generally known for sockets and wrenches, but we sell much more than that," said Wayne King, who became president of the division in 1995.

> *"Specialty tools, fastener application tools, tools that are used on everything from construction to pipe-lines, to mining, gas and oil refineries. We are very large in the resource industry. We have products that are used on space shuttle construction, so we are anywhere from thousands of miles in the air to several hundred feet below the ground, when we get into mining applications."[17]*

Richard H. Ayers, currently chief executive officer of The Stanley Works, became executive vice president in 1984.

paign chairman for the United Way, chairman of the Boy's Club Fund Drive, past president of the New Britain Board of Education, an officer of the National Association of Manufacturers (where he would serve as chairman from 1987 to 1989), a trustee of the Connecticut Business and Industry Association, a member of the governing body of The Conference Board, and a regent of the University of Hartford.[14]

The year ended on a positive financial note as well, with record sales of $1.16 billion and earnings of $73.4 million.[15]

Also in 1984, Stanley acquired HED vehicle-mounted hydraulic tools, which became part of the Hydraulic Tools Division.[18]

Richard H. Ayers

In 1984, Richard H. Ayers was elected to the position of executive vice president, reporting to President Arthur Gledhill.[19] The following year, Gledhill retired and Ayers was elected chief operating officer and president of The Stanley Works. Ayers grew up in Massachusetts and attended the Massachusetts Institute of Technology, where he received both his bachelor's and his master's degree. He joined Stanley in 1972 as a project manager for the Stanley Tools Division. As president, Ayers wasted no time improving the bottom line of The Stanley Works, as a 1985 stock recommendation from First Boston Research indicates.

"Stanley Works, a company virtually synonymous with tools and hardware, is seeking to position itself for a burst of growth in both sales and earnings. The company was hit hard by the recession. ... Now, however, Stanley is pressing ahead with cost-reduction programs. Mr. Ayers, the new president, is actively involved in all aspects of the business. And the Proto, Mac and Vidmar acquisitions all appear to be doing well, indicating that management is willing to buy

Stanley's World Headquarters, constructed in 1984, firmly re-established New Britain, Connecticut, as the Hardware City of the World.

smaller businesses at reasonable prices and nurture them."[20]

To help consolidate operations, Stanley in 1986 divested four companies, Stanley Steel—U.S., Stanley Precision Steel in Canada, Stanley Strapping Systems and Stanley Structures. The company also acquired seven companies that year, helping to boost sales by 36 percent.[21]

The first major acquisition of 1986 was the Bostitch fastener and fastening tool business, which was purchased from Textron Inc. for approximately $200 million.[22] The new division, Stanley-Bostitch, made not only staplers for the home and office, but a wide range of fastening tools for assembly operations, furniture and manufacturing, bindery stitchers and air-powered tools.

The company enjoyed an easy transition learning to fit in with the corporate culture of The Stanley Works. John Turpin, who was with Bostitch at the time of the acquisition, said, "It was a very positive experience for all of us at Bostitch. In terms of the people, the way that we melded with The Stanley Works, it couldn't have been finer."[23] Turpin later became president of the Air Tools Division and is now vice president of operations for The Stanley Works.

Later in the year, Stanley purchased the hand tools business of the Peugeot group in France; ESSCORP, a leader in design, manufacture and installation of automated material storage and retrieval systems; the Hartco Company, supplier of specialty tools and fasteners, which became part of the Stanley-Bostitch Division; Sutton-Landis, supplier of shoe repair tools and fasteners; Halstead Enterprises, Inc., manufacturer of collated nails; and National Hand Tool Corporation, a leader in design and manufacturing technology of mechanic's hand tools for Do-It-Yourselfers and professionals.[24]

In 1986, Stanley ran a television commercial that depicted a woman using Stanley products to convert a loft into a photography studio. It was the first Stanley advertisement to show a woman completing a Do-It-Yourself project without any help. Ayers explained why the advertisement was important to The Stanley Works.

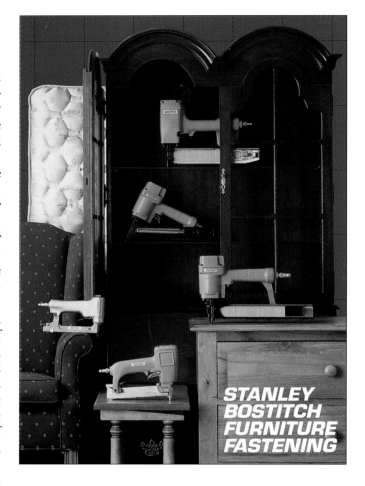

The Stanley Works created the Stanley-Bostitch division in 1986, after it acquired the Bostitch fastener and fastening tool company.

Right: This 1986 television commercial was the first Stanley advertisement to show a woman completing a Do-It-Yourself project by herself.

"We were saying in a subtle way that women can take on Do-It-Yourself projects and be successful at it. We firmly believe that. There is a market there. It is interesting that we received several letters from women who said, 'Thank God, someone's finally recognized that we can do projects too!'"[25]

In 1987, Stanley acquired three new companies: Acme General Corporation, which produced sliding and folding door hardware; Plan-A-Flex, the originator of an inexpensive and accurate way to create home construction and remodeling plans; and Beach Industries, Inc., manufacturer of metal tool boxes and related products for professional mechanics and Do-It-Yourselfers.[26]

Stanley Home Automation

Stanley Automatic Openers Division changed its name to Stanley Home Automation in 1987 and introduced The Stanley Lightmaker, which allowed a homeowner to open the garage door and turn on lights inside and outside the house, while never leaving the comfort of the car.[27] Innovative products such as the Lightmaker help the division set itself apart from its competitors, which include Sears and Genie. Joseph Jones, who became president and general manager of Stanley Home Automation in 1989, and is now president of Stanley Tools North America, said one of Home Automation's biggest challenges is the seasonal changes in sales.

"If somebody made it through the winter with a garage door opener that didn't work right, they wouldn't replace it in the spring because the weather was nice and it was light at night and security was better. They tended to postpone the purchase. But when the weather turned cold, they'd say, 'Gee, I've lived with that situation long enough. I'm going to replace that broken or faulty garage door opener.' So you kind of went through the first half of the year holding your breath and wondering if all that business was going to come in. Planning was always a challenge."[28]

In 1988, Stanley acquired the specialty tool and fastener business of Spenax, which became part of the Stanley-Bostitch Division.[29] The following year, Stanley acquired The Parker Group, manufacturer of fastening products including glue guns and riveting tools, and introduced its line of Steel Plank closet organizers.[30]

YOU'RE DOING IT RIGHT.

Stanley quality improves the quality of your life.

Stanley's new "Loft" commercial has a dramatic new look to appeal to a new generation of female do-it-yourselfers.

ANNCR: It's just a loft.

Just a dirty old loft,

unless you know what to do with it.

SINGERS: YOU'RE DOING IT RIGHT.

YOU'RE DOING IT RIGHT.

YOU'RE DOING IT . . .

DOING IT . . .

YOU'RE DOING IT RIGHT.

YOU'RE DOING IT RIGHT.

'CAUSE IT MEANS MORE WHEN YOU'RE DOING IT FOR YOURSELF.

ANNCR: Stanley. For the quality of your life.

SINGERS: STANLEY HELPS YOU DO THINGS RIGHT.

Stanley has developed such a strong presence in England that many British consider it an English company. Inset: A double-decker bus advertises Stanley products. Above: A Mac tools truck drives in front of the London House of Parliament.

CHAPTER THIRTEEN

GROWING AROUND THE WORLD

"My philosophy has been to position Stanley in more and more markets around the world and to do it in a careful way so that we don't bet the success of the company by doing something foolish in a market we don't understand."

— CEO Richard H. Ayers[1]

AFTER A REMARKABLE 21 years as chief executive officer of The Stanley Works, Donald Davis stepped down from the position in 1987. His successor was Richard Ayers, who had been rising through the ranks of The Stanley Works since he was hired in 1972. "For a good year and a half or two years before he was CEO, I talked about it publicly," Davis recalled. "I started building him up for the job way ahead of the time it was announced."[2]

In May 1989, Davis retired from the chairmanship, and Ayers filled that position as well.[3] When Davis stepped down, business and political leaders throughout Connecticut praised his contributions as both a businessman and a citizen. "Don Davis is the quintessential chief executive — dynamic, impatient with anything that falls short of excellence in business or in community service," said William B. Ellis, chairman and CEO of Northeast Utilities. "Under his guidance, The Stanley Works has developed a unique and effective approach to good corporate citizenship — one in which employee involvement goes hand-in-hand with corporate giving."[4]

Connecticut Congresswoman Nancy Johnson expressed similar sentiments.

"I know Don as a friend and colleague, and have long respected his commitment, sincerity and devotion to family. On matters of business, government, and service to the community, he has led the way with enthusiasm and results. Don never asks more than he is willing to give — but that's always 150 percent. His thoughtful leadership at Stanley, in major community and state organizations, as a strong president of the National Association of Manufacturers and as a creative international businessman has been an example to business and community leaders alike."[5]

Ayers noted that every CEO in Stanley's long history has made the company stronger and more successful. As the current chief executive, he hopes to do the same.

"In each case, there has been a hand-off of a more successful company than when they joined it, and that's what I'd like to accomplish as well. I happen to be at a time in Stanley history where some of the external influences are a little more dramatic than they were in the past. The time horizon to be able to respond to those influences

Above: Introduced in 1963, Stanley's convenient and durable Powerlock rules are still the best-selling rules in the world.

is shorter than it has been, so there has been some urgency to develop an organization that is leaner and more responsive to the changing conditions of the marketplace.

"I have been trying to enlist everybody in that competitive process. We're trying to get more people involved, so that everybody is bringing ideas to the table and making improvements. I hope people will look back and say that my key contribution has been to really open up the place, so everybody feels they are part of meeting that competitive challenge. That's the key, because no one person is going to make or break The Stanley Works, but an awful lot of people can help make it successful."[6]

Ayers got off to a strong start. Both 1988 and 1989 were record years for The Stanley Works, and the company finished the decade with sales of nearly $2 billion and earnings of $117.7 million. To increase its presence in the rapidly growing Asian market, The Stanley Works established a manufacturing and business base in Taiwan.[7]

Richard H. Ayers and Donald W. Davis review a display of Stanley tools.

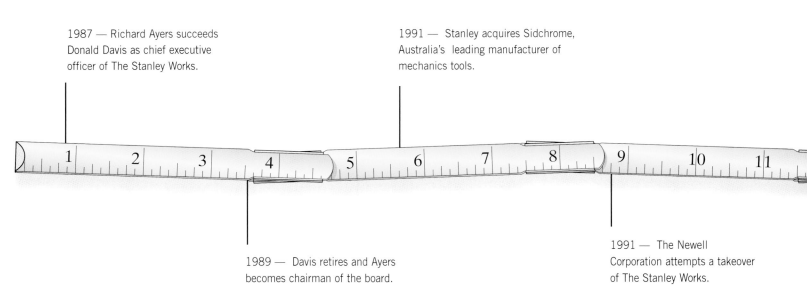

1987 — Richard Ayers succeeds Donald Davis as chief executive officer of The Stanley Works.

1991 — Stanley acquires Sidchrome, Australia's leading manufacturer of mechanics tools.

1989 — Davis retires and Ayers becomes chairman of the board.

1991 — The Newell Corporation attempts a takeover of The Stanley Works.

Richard Ayers succeeded Davis as chief executive officer of The Stanley Works in 1987, and became chairman when Davis retired in 1989.

The initiative showed immediate results. International business increased to 28 percent of sales in 1988, up from 22 percent in1987.[8]

The Nineties

In the 1989 Annual Report, Ayers noted that the coming decade would pose new challenges for The Stanley Works.

"We will meet these challenges by continuing to deliver the extra measure of value that is expected of Stanley — quality products, a preferred brand, outstanding customer service, world-class manufacturing. We know that the new decade will require dedicated people who understand complex political and economic challenges and who can convert these challenges into leadership opportunities for Stanley."[9]

Despite this optimism, the nineties began on a low note, with a 9 percent drop in net earnings. The 1990 Annual Report attributed the drop to "declining, then recessionary market conditions in Australia, Canada, the United States and the United Kingdom," and the Iraqi invasion of Kuwait, which "further reduced consumer confidence."[10]

The following year did not show much improvement. "For the second year in a row, weak economies in many countries of the world adversely affected our businesses," noted the

1992 — Newell agrees to drop the takeover attempt.

1992 — Stanley acquires Mail Media, marketer of precision tools through catalogs.

1992 — Stanley acquires Goldblatt Tool Company, manufacturer of masonry, tile and drywall tools.

1991 Annual Report. Earnings dropped 11 percent, yet the company continued to take steps toward securing its future. It remained committed to international expansion, and was rewarded with a 20 percent increase in sales to Asian markets. Stanley also forged a joint-venture agreement to create Stanley Poland Ltd., which manufactured tools in the newly opened markets

Above: A hardware store in downtown Hong Kong proudly displays an enormous neon image of one of Stanley's familiar hand tools.

Left: The universally recognizable Stanley logo stands out among dozens of street signs on a busy street in Taiwan. In the late eighties, Stanley established a manufacturing and business base in Taiwan to take advantage of the rapidly growing Asian market.

of Eastern Europe. In addition, a record number of new products were introduced in 1991.[11]

The Stanley Works acquired five companies in 1991, the majority of which furthered the company's goal of international growth. The acquired companies included Nirva, a French fabricator and distributor of closet systems; Mosley-Stone, a British manufacturer of paint preparation tools, paintbrushes and applicators; J.B. Supplies, an American distributor of drapery hardware and decorator products; Sidchrome, an Australian manufacturer of mechanics tools; and Monarch, an American manufacturer of sliding and bi-fold mirrored-doors.[12] John Francis, president and general manager of Stanley Tools Australia and New Zealand, noted that Sidchrome led the Australian market in mechanics tools when it was acquired by Stanley.[13]

In a 1995 interview, Ayers discussed his goals for Stanley's continued international expansion.

"My philosophy has been to position Stanley in more and more markets around the world, and to do it in a careful way, so that we don't bet the

success of the company by doing something foolish in a market we don't understand. We tend to go in and develop a selling relationship with existing distribution, often with our existing products, so we can learn about the markets. Then, perhaps, we'll support it with warehouses, and add some manufacturing behind that."[14]

This strategy has been employed in Thailand, Indonesia, Singapore, China and India, among other places.

Stanley's Universal Appeal

The worldwide growth of The Stanley Works is bolstered by the fact that Stanley products are favored by professionals and Do-It-Yourselfers around the world. The Stanley Works has such a strong presence in Europe that many people mistakenly believe it is a British company. "We have been in Europe since the turn of the century," said Patricia McLean, manager of corporate communications. "In England, most people don't know that Stanley isn't a British company. That kind of brand recognition helps some of our business units very much."[15]

C. Stewart Gentsch, who retired in 1995 as president and general manager of Stanley Tools Worldwide, was struck, during a recent visit to Singapore, by the universal popularity of Stanley tools.

"There is a bridge from Malaysia into Singapore. ... The light changed, and across the bridge came all these guys on motor scooters. I mean, 200 of them at once going around this corner. I looked, and I saw about 10 guys with contractor-grade tape rulers hanging on their belts. These are Malaysian workers that probably made $2 a day, and they had the very best Stanley tools money could buy. ... Later in the day, we went to visit a local retailer, and he gave us basically the same story. He said, 'Your products are very expensive,

but when I put them in the hands of a professional, they use it in their trade and they come back for more. They're not concerned about the price. They want the features and benefits of the contractor grade."[16]

The Stanley Works is also popular in Latin America, said Robert Hudson, director of marketing for Stanley Tools Latin America since 1993. "It's amazing how positive our customers are about the company, the products that we sell, and the lines that we offer. It really makes me feel proud."[17]

Though the Stanley brand name has universal appeal, there are substantial cultural differences among tool users. Hudson noted that many Stanley tools are created for specific regional needs.

"It is our strategy to be competitive worldwide in the products we make. If you look at our Brazilian operation, we are very good at making panel blades, hacksaw blades, hacksaw frames and some squares. If you go to Colombia, we are essentially making machetes for the agricultural side of our business. In Mexico, we do some forged products, hammers, things of that nature, as well as hand planes."[18]

Gentsch noted that tools in Europe are configured with different needs in mind.

"Hammers in Europe are altogether different. They don't use claw hammers because, for the most part, construction in Central Europe is masonry. They have to drive masonry nails or bolts, so they need a relatively heavy hammer. A screwdriver in Europe is never used as a chisel or to open a paint can or as a pry bar. So the screwdrivers are finer, more delicate. People are very careful

Two young boys in Thailand proudly hold aloft their Stanley hammers.

The international growth of The Stanley Works would not be possible without the hard work and dedication of employees throughout the world.

Above right: The European team of the Stanley Tools Division posed for this informal photograph in the late eighties.

Below right: R. Alan Hunter and Richard Ayers enjoy a night on the town with the company's Singapore team during a 1989 visit.

with their tools, and they store them properly and put them away when they're not using them. Not like us Americans, who stir paint with screwdrivers and things like that."[19]

The Competitive Edge

These cultural differences add an interesting challenge to the ongoing process of streamlining operations, said Joseph L. Jones, who was vice president of sales and marketing for Stanley Tools in the late eighties, and is now president of Stanley Tools North America.

"One of the things we did was look at the major product lines. Instead of having three manufacturing locations for tape rules, we decided we would consolidate everything in France. We went through the product line with this philosophy. The interesting

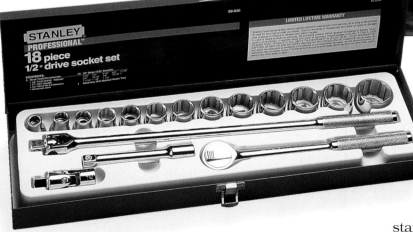

A wrench set from Stanley's Mechanics Tools Division.

thing about that whole exercise was that we had to spend a good deal of time sitting around a table getting people to agree on designs. We wanted to come up with a design that would work for all of Europe. ... As a result we really did standardize a great deal of product offerings in Europe during that period of time."[20]

As Stanley grows around the world, it is constantly finding ways to improve the efficiency of operations, noted Hudson.

"Latin America used to have protected markets. Now that the borders are down and the duty rates have dropped, it is a lot more competitive. We need to be much more competitive with our manufacturing in those countries. We used to make a very broad range of Stanley tools, using some discarded equipment that Stanley had in its U.S. operations many years ago. About three years ago, we started consolidating into one factory and trying to upgrade the equipment and processes. We discontinued some products altogether and imported them from other Stanley locations around the world."[21]

Do-It-Yourself products are gaining popularity around the world. This easy-to-install garage door opener is a popular item in Germany.

In sparsely populated regions, such as Australia and New Zealand, operating costs must be kept low because the sales volume is smaller than in other places, said John Francis, president of hand tools and general manager for Australia and New Zealand since 1984. Stanley tools are popular in these countries because the mild climate encourages Do-It-Yourself projects. The Stanley Tools Division has four manufacturing facilities in Australia. The major plant, as well as the headquarters, are in Heidelberg, a suburb of Melbourne. The New Zealand operation consists of about 15 people, Francis said.[22]

One way The Stanley Works is streamlining operations in Europe is through the creation of a sophisticated financial system similar to the zero-balance system it uses in the United States, said Chief Financial Officer Richard Huck. The system allows The Stanley Works to improve its investment opportunities by concentrating its resources in one place.

"Since there are different currencies in Europe, it would not be as easily done there as it is in the United States. We challenged one of the major banks in the world to put that in place for us. They agreed, and then quickly realized they had never done this before. At first, they thought they had bitten off more than they could chew. Then they agreed that they were committed to it and so they were going to do it. We would perhaps be the first company that has ever

Catalogs from Jensen and Direct Safety are printed in several languages

Connecticut Attorney General Richard Blumenthal (left) and Stanley Works CEO Richard Ayers announce that Newell has dropped its takeover bid of The Stanley Works.

done this, and they would like to be the ones to pull it off. I think we're staying on the cutting edge of things in this area."[23]

Of course, streamlining can never take the place of the world-class quality of Stanley products. Carl Stoutenberg, product line engineering manager for Stanley Tools, and unofficial historian for the division, said part of his job is to make sure all Stanley tools meet the company's high standards.

"Stanley has gone out and established manufacturing facilities throughout the world over the years. My job is to make sure that even though it's coming from across the sea somewhere, it is still made to Stanley's demanding standards. We get involved with the inspection of these tools and the specifications of these tools to make sure they are what we feel should carry the Stanley name."[24]

The Newell Threat

Throughout the long history of The Stanley Works, the company has never attempted to acquire a company that did not want to become part of the Stanley family. So Stanley executives were surprised when their company was the target of an undesired takeover attempt by the Newell Corporation. The acquisition overtures started out friendly, but quickly changed tone, recalled CEO Ayers, who was president at the time.

"These are people we have known in the industry for years and years. In fact, [Newell CEO] Dan Fergusen and [Stanley Chairman] Don Davis had known each other for a very long time. That's how it started. Dan Fergusen asked if we could sit down and talk about what the array of business opportunities might be.

"We explored lots of different options and decided that there wasn't anything that made sense and wouldn't create a risk for both companies. We were into that rip-roaring period where lots of hostile merger and acquisition activities were occurring, and we didn't want to be vulnerable to that.

"So, after going through all that, I got a phone call announcing that Newell had acquired some of our shares and would be moving ahead to see

what else they might do to complete some kind of business arrangement with Stanley. ... I heard it from Dan Fergusen, but it was concurrent with the fact that they had already acquired the stock, and they were about to make a filing with the Justice Department, and he was simply telling me what they had done.

"As I have said consistently throughout the whole thing, the most discouraging aspect of the whole process was that any conversation that had taken place with them, I thought was friendly and private, and they acted unfriendly and public with their actions."[25]

In a 1992 letter to employees, Ayers discussed the many reasons why Stanley opposed the acquisition.

"Not only would it violate federal and Connecticut antitrust laws, it would also fail to serve the best interests of Stanley shareholders, customers, employees and other constituencies and could, in fact, harm the company and those to which it is responsible. ... Lacking its own brand name and the leverage with merchants such an asset offers, Newell now seeks to seize the one we've built and cultivated for over a century, and is not particular about its methods."[26]

Above: A Spanish advertisement for Stanley tools.

A collection of machetes manufactured by Collins Company of Latin America, acquired by The Stanley Works in 1966.

The struggle between Newell and Stanley continued for about nine months. In the end, The Stanley Works triumphed, in large part because Connecticut's attorney general filed a lawsuit parallel to the one filed by Stanley. Battling the state agency was more than Newell had bargained for, Ayers said.[27]

Stanley also fought the acquisition attempt by purchasing American Brush Company, Inc., a firm that manufactures paintbrushes and decorator tools. Although American Brush was purchased for its own merits, the acquisition created an area of overlap with Newell that represented a potential Federal Trade Commission violation.

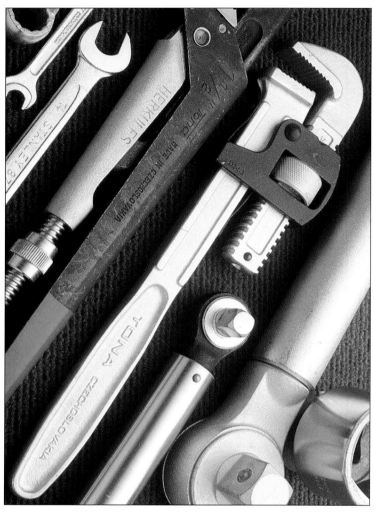

Tona a.s. Pecky, a Czechoslovakian manufacturer of mechanics tools, was acquired by The Stanley Works in 1992.

Stanley's antitrust case was also bolstered by the fact that Newell had acquired Anchor Hocking, the glass and plastics company that had purchased Amerock from Stanley in 1972, Ayers said.

"The government had said that because of antitrust reasons, we were not permitted to keep Amerock. And now Newell owns that business. How can Newell put that back into Stanley and expect everything to be fine? The lawyers told me that times have changed, and the government might not view that as being as serious an overlap as it was when we were forced to divest it.

But clearly any area of overlap that could be identified would add to the frustration of Newell." [28]

The combination of the antitrust issues and the lawsuit filed by Connecticut's attorney general finally convinced Newell to abandon the acquisition attempt, Ayers recalled.

"It was a surprise ending. Their general counsel approached our general counsel late one day and asked how we could end this thing. Our general counsel said, 'We could end it by having you go away.' And their guy said, 'Well, how can we arrange that?' As it turned out, the key stumbling block in putting it all together was taking care of the attorney general's office. So we not only had to get Newell to agree on a standstill against Stanley for some period of time, but also making a payment to the attorney general's office to defray some of the legal cost he had put into the battle.

"My worry was that the deal might come apart. But as it turned out, I talked with the attorney general and said, 'If it comes down to having this deal fall apart because of what you're trying to do in getting your legal fees covered, would you be willing to step away from that demand?' He said, 'Yes.' And I said, 'Let's stick with it a little bit longer.' It turned out that he got part of what he was looking for and we got the right conclusion." [29]

The agreement reached in court required Newell to sell its holdings of less than 1 percent of Stanley stock within a reasonable period not to exceed one year, that Newell would not purchase any additional Stanley securities "or seek to control or influence Stanley for 10 years, and that antitrust litigation would be terminated." [30]

An editorial in the *New Britain Herald* described the takeover attempt as "one of the most dangerous chapters in Stanley's long and storied history."

"Mr. Ayers personally deserves a great deal of credit for fighting Newell. No doubt he was offered or would have been offered some attractive incentives. Instead, he resisted, choosing instead to keep his company independent. Other executives, in similar positions in Connecticut, have not displayed such courage and loyalty." [31]

Important Acquisitions

Although it seemed as though the Newell battle dominated everybody's calendar in 1992, Stanley still had time to do what it does best — manufacture and sell high-quality products. That year, sales exceeded $2 billion for the first time in Stanley's history.[32]

Always innovative in marketing methods, The Stanley Works in 1992 found new ways to merchandise special woodworking tools made by Stanley Tools in England, France and Poland. "We realized there was a woodworking market," said Donna Alexander, manager of marketing communications. "It's worked out quite well for us, and sales have been climbing ever since."[33]

The company placed three advertisements in *American Woodworker* magazine, and the response was phenomenal, she said. The success of this niche marketing prompted her department to create individual catalogs targeted toward particular markets, including fine woodworking, painting and contractor-grade tools.

Alexander said niche marketing will continue to grow as the company learns more about particular users and the products they want to buy. Products will be modified to meet the needs of these specialized markets, she noted.

In 1992, Stanley continued to acquire compatible companies. In addition to American Brush, Stanley's acquisitions included the Goldblatt Tool Company, which manufactured masonry, tile and drywall tools, and Mail Media, which consisted of Jensen Tools, Inc. and Direct Safety, which marketed precision tools through catalogs. Stanley also acquired a controlling interest in Tona a.s. Pecky, a major Czech manufacturer of mechanics tools, and LaBounty Manufacturing, Inc., a manufacturer of large hydraulic tools.

"Stanley had long been interested in acquiring Goldblatt," said Joseph

Jones. "That was a business we had on our wish list for a number of years, and they actually came to us. It was perfect. It was an opportunity for us to go after a business that was certainly complementary to our business."[34] Mail Media has provided a valuable new direction for Stanley in the line of catalog sales.

One important advantage of acquiring and integrating these companies is that Stanley can market a complete line of products to a retail outlet, said Alexander. The acquisition of American Brush is one example. "If you are at the store buying paint, you typically go for the paint and then you buy whatever applications products they have on hand. We are now able to sell both the tools and the paint accessory product, and bring some marketing into that," she said.[35]

"In the case of Goldblatt, it was a matter of us being able to offer further service to a Home Depot or another home center or hardware store and say, 'You're buying a lot of Stanley tools for your carpentry needs. Look what else we're offering. High-end masonry and tile tools. You can order it now from the same company.'"[36]

Alexander said the new companies were easy to integrate into the Stanley culture, because the companies shared values that are important to Stanley. "I've met a lot of folks from Goldblatt, and they are just like us — hard-working people who get out there and sell the best product they can to the customer and service the heck out of them," she said.[37]

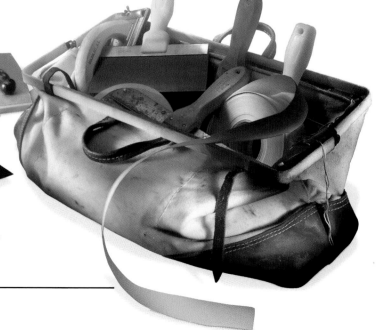

The Goldblatt Tool Company of Kansas City, Kansas, acquired by Stanley in 1992, manufactures masonry and tile tools.

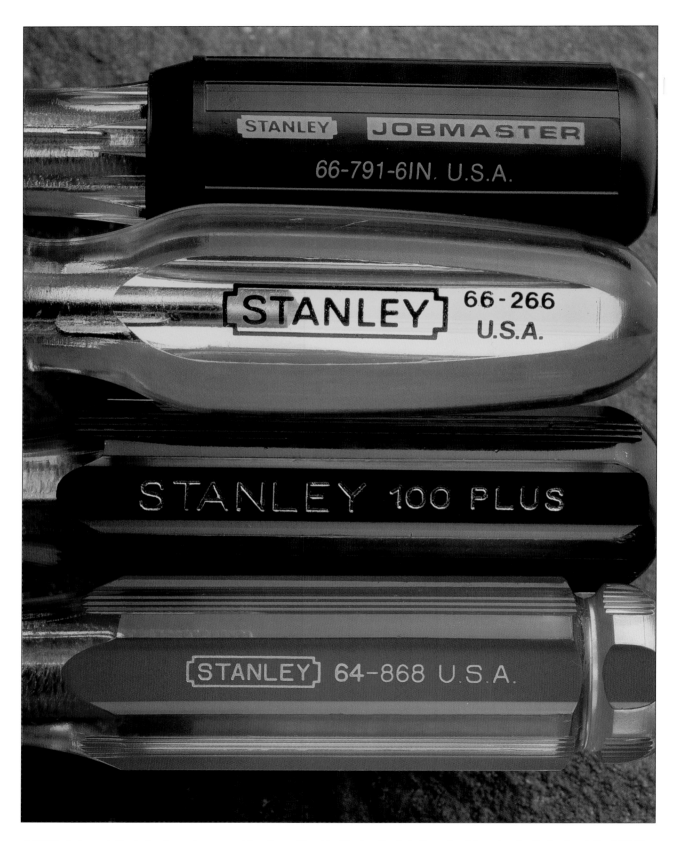

A 1990 photograph illustrates the various screwdriver lines offered by Stanley. Top to bottom: the Jobmaster, the Professional, the 100 Plus and the Handyman.

CHAPTER FOURTEEN

PLANNING FOR THE FUTURE

"We are proud of our heritage, but we will not rest on our reputation. We believe that constantly striving to be the world's best at what we do is the only way we can keep our reputation for excellence."

— *Proud of Our Past, 1993*[1]

THE STANLEY WORKS celebrated its 150th anniversary in 1993 with the theme, "Proud of Our Past, Focused on Our Future." The company introduced a commemorative collection of classic Stanley hand tools and held a Family Day in the summer, which included a free outdoor concert in New Britain. The company also set up a showroom of Stanley memorabilia and prepared a booklet and video about its long history.

The Stanley Works had come a long way from the one-story wooden building that Frederick T. Stanley had purchased in 1843. It had become a global manufacturer and marketer of tools and hardware, with sales of $2.3 billion and a work force of 18,500 people. But in fundamental ways, The Stanley Works had changed very little. "The principles of doing business handed down to us by our founder, Frederick T. Stanley, are the same principles that will be the foundation of success for our future," proclaimed the anniversary booklet.

"Value. Provide superior value to our customers. Respect. Treat people with understanding and respect. Integrity. Plain, old fashioned honesty. Quality. The glue that holds Stanley together. We are proud of our heritage, but we will not

rest on our reputation. We believe that constantly striving to be the world's best at what we do is the only way we can keep our reputation for excellence."[2]

A Year of Record Sales

In June 1993, R. Alan Hunter became president and chief operating officer of The Stanley Works. Hunter had graduated from Dickinson College in 1968 with a degree in economics, and had served in the Navy for three and a half years. He earned his MBA at the University of Pennsylvania's Wharton School, and, upon graduation in 1974, he joined the two-year management training program at The Stanley Works. He soon grew impatient with the program, however, and asked to leave, arguing that his military experience had already prepared him for a management role.[3]

Hunter's request was granted and he was assigned to the Hand Tools Division. From there, he moved up the ranks to become controller of Air Tools in 1980, corporate vice president in charge of finance in 1986, and chief financial officer the

Above: To celebrate the company's 150th anniversary, The Stanley Works in 1993 offered a special line of commemorative tools.

following year. When he became president of The Stanley Works in 1993, Richard Ayers remained chairman and CEO.[4]

The Stanley Works posted record sales of nearly $2.3 billion in 1993. Part of the growth could be attributed to new acquisitions, including Friess & Company KG, a German manufacturer and marketer of paint rollers and brushes, and Rikko-Sha Company, Ltd., a Japanese mechanics tools distributor.[5] New manufacturing facilities in Malaysia and Indonesia increased Stanley's expansion into the Asian market. The Stanley Works expanded its facility in Thailand, adding the manufacture of hardware and a more complete line of hand tools.[6]

The same year, The Stanley Works moved its pneumatic fastening tool line out of Japan, said CFO Richard Huck.

"We made that transition at just about the right time. We started as the yen started to move, and fortunately we made the conversion before we really took it on the chin in terms of the differential

R. Alan Hunter, president of The Stanley Works since 1993.

between the dollar and the yen. In hindsight, looking back where we were five years ago, and looking at where we are today, I would rather have those products made in the United States than in Japan."[7]

Also in 1993, Stanley sold the franchise operations of Taylor Rental, its wholly owned subsidiary, and in 1994, the related company-owned stores were sold as well.[8]

Sales in 1994 topped $2.5 billion for the first time in Stanley history, partly because of continued international expansion. That year, Stanley's growing international reputation paid off when the company won a contract to supply hinges for the world's tallest building, the twin Petronas towers in Kuala Lumpur, Malaysia.[9]

In a reorganization, Stanley consolidated 23 divisions into 11, which included Stanley Tools, Stanley Mechanics Tools, Mail Media, Stanley Air Tools, Stanley Hydraulic Tools, Stanley Fastening Systems, Stanley Hardware, Stanley Storage Systems, Stanley Door Systems, Stanley Access Technologies, and Stanley Acmetrack, which, in 1995, became part of the new Stanley Home Decor Division. All divisions were given the responsibility to represent their products around the world.

Stanley Tools

With more than 9,000 products, including rules, hammers, planes, levels, tool boxes, paintbrushes, trowels and much more, the Stanley Tools Division is the largest manufacturer of hand tools in the world.

C. Stewart Gentsch became president and general manager of Stanley Tools Worldwide as part of the reorganization. Hired by The Stanley Works in 1982, he became vice president of manufacturing in 1984, and president of the Domestic Tools Division in 1985.

The Stanley Tools Division dates back to 1853, with the establishment of Hall & Knapp, the company that merged with A. Stanley & Company in 1857 to form the Stanley Rule & Level Company. The Stanley Works acquired the Stanley Rule & Level Company in 1920. Even though the division is mature, Joseph Jones, president of Stanley Tools North America, believes it has tremendous growth potential.

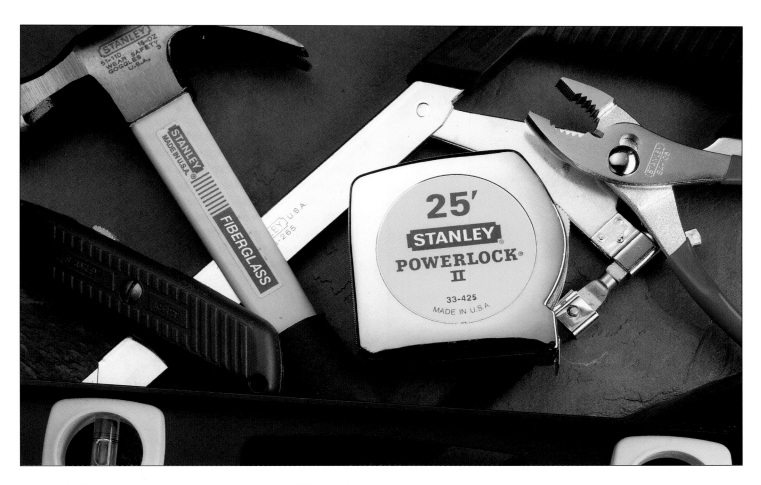

A selection of popular Stanley tools, showcased for a 1993 promotion.

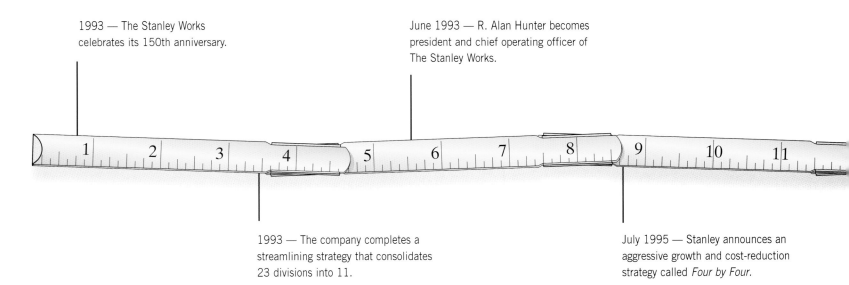

1993 — The Stanley Works celebrates its 150th anniversary.

June 1993 — R. Alan Hunter becomes president and chief operating officer of The Stanley Works.

1993 — The company completes a streamlining strategy that consolidates 23 divisions into 11.

July 1995 — Stanley announces an aggressive growth and cost-reduction strategy called *Four by Four*.

Above: Stanley Hardware, the oldest division of The Stanley Works, still manufactures the bolts, hinges and brackets that first made Stanley famous.

Right: Efficient storage systems are the hallmark of Stanley-Vidmar, a brand name within the Stanley Storage Systems Division.

Stanley Hardware

The Stanley Hardware Division manufactures and markets more than 12,000 products, including hinges, bolts, reinforcement hardware, shelf brackets, latches, and engineered components for the appliance industry.

The hardware business is almost totally North American, with only 4 percent of the business international, said Henning Kornbrekke, division president. "It grew up in the United States and spread throughout North America, but never beyond that," he said, adding that efforts are under way to improve international business.[16] The division manufactures in Canada and two locations in the United States, and it shares a manufacturing facility in Thailand with the tool division.

Since it manufactures the founding products of The Stanley Works, the Hardware Division has the unique challenge of finding ways to update a business that developed more than 150 years ago, Kornbrekke said.[17]

Stanley Hardware includes the Engineered Components business unit, which manufactures hardware components for the appliance industry, explained Patrick Egan, unit president. "We manufacture latches for self-cleaning ovens, hinges for oven door use, and various tools and metal pieces that can be used on other appliances. We do custom designs, working closely with our customers to design a product unique to them."[18]

Egan said the future looks bright for Engineered Components. "In the next three years, I think there are going to be some good opportunities for us, probably in the appliance industry because that's where we have the best

These inventory storage products are among the items offered by Stanley Storage Systems.

contacts. ... There is really no competitor who can supply all of the components. There are competitors in each of the lines, but nobody is out there that can do all of it."[19]

Stanley Storage Systems

This division provides cabinets, racks and engineered handling systems for inventory control, storage and retrieval. Products in this division are available as Stanley-Vidmar in North and South America, and as Stanley Storage Systems in Asia. The storage products are designed for maximum efficiency, providing significant reductions in the amount of space needed for the storage of parts, supplies and tools.

The division works closely with customers to meet specific handling and storage needs, offer creative solutions that include secure storage, customized work stations, and retrieval systems that consistently provide quick, easy access to the tools and parts that customers use.

Stanley Door Systems

Stanley Door Systems manufactures and markets a complete line of entry doors, garage

doors, garage door openers, gate operators and radio controls. Dick Dandurand, president of the division since 1994, said Stanley doors are popular with Do-It-Yourselfers because Stanley provides all the tools and hardware needed for installation. "Our strength is in combination with the major home centers and lumber yards around the country," he said. "It's a great combination for Stanley to continue to grow."[20]

The division recently introduced the Weather-Wise Door System, an extremely durable door that won't warp, crack or rot. One of the division's most interesting recent projects was the development of Homelink, a joint activity with the Prince Corporation. Similar to a remote control for a television, Homelink allows the user to activate home appliances from the car, so it would be possible, for example, to turn on the lights, get the coffee started and perhaps adjust the air conditioning before entering the house, Dandurand said. "It has been featured in the advertisements of a number of different car manufacturers and it

Stanley Door Systems offers the most attractive, energy-efficient and weather-resistant residential doors on the market.

The Access Technologies Division produces the most efficient and innovative automatic doors in the world.

really looks like it's going to take hold and become standard equipment in higher-end cars."[21]

Stanley Access Technologies

Ever since The Stanley Works introduced the first Magic Door in 1930, Stanley has set the industry standard for automatic doors. Today, the Access Technologies Division manufactures, sells and services automatic doors and parking systems worldwide. The division doubled its business between 1990 and 1995, said Kornbrekke, who was president of the division until 1995, when he became president of the Hardware Division.[22]

Tom Jones, who succeeded Kornbrekke as president of the division, said the Magic Door improved dramatically since it was first introduced.

"In those days, and even into the early fifties, automatic doors were $10,000 a pair. It was usually pneumatically operated, which meant you had to install an air compressor and air line. Today, a comparable product would cost about $3,500, and you would get a very reliable product that probably wouldn't have to be touched, other than for routine service, for five years.

"With the older product, I always believed it was the cost of ownership that kept people from moving to automatic doors. You might have to repair it three, four, five times a year."[23]

The division also provides doors for transportation systems, primarily in trains. Shuttle systems in the Newark, Cincinnati and Orlando airports, for example, use Stanley doors that open and shut automatically. And it is involved in providing security systems based on magnetic cards that are used to open doors, Kornbrekke said.[24]

Stanley Home Decor

The Stanley Home Decor Division was created in July 1995 by combining the decorative mirror, mirror door, and closet storage products groups from Stanley Hardware with Stanley Acmetrack, which manufactured bi-fold and sliding closet doors and organizing systems. Raymond J. Martino, formerly vice president of operations at Stanley Hardware, was appointed president and general manager of the new division.[25]

The new division reflects Stanley's increasing presence in the home decorating products category worldwide.

The Changing Global Marketplace

All the divisions of The Stanley Works are adjusting to a rapidly changing retail landscape.

Stanley sales people used to sell their products to mom-and-pop hardware stores through distributors. Today, Stanley's largest customers are giant retail chains such as Home Depot, Lowe's and Wal-Mart. The competition for these important customers is fierce, noted Joseph Jones, president of Stanley Tools North America. "If Stanley wants to maintain and grow its market share position, it will have to become more aggressive in terms of new products and pricing and costs," he said. "If we are not, then somebody is going to take that business from us."[26]

These retailers are also very sophisticated in picking and choosing among products, noted CEO Ayers, adding, "they don't necessarily buy the entire tool program from one supplier."[27]

One way that Stanley keeps ahead of the competition is by listening to end user customers, and constantly developing new products to meet their particular needs. CEO Ayers gave the example of a crimping tool that was designed to solve a customer's problem.

"We have a crimping tool that is hydraulically driven. It is used by electric utility companies when they are trying to crimp a very large connector on a large diameter cable. They were having difficulty doing that with traditional methods, and they needed some sort of mechanically assisted device to do the crimping. We created a very clever hydraulically driven crimping tool that, just by depressing the trigger, comes in and crimps the connector into the cable."[28]

Ayers reflected that it's only a matter of time before the large retail chains become global entities. Home Depot, Wal-Mart and Kmart have already started opening stores outside the United States, he said. "I really believe that the same trends we are seeing here are going to be seen in markets around the world."[29]

Robert Hudson, director of marketing for Stanley Tools Latin America, said he sees evidence of the trend in Latin American countries.

"We have started seeing some of the mass merchants in our territories. They all wanted to start with Mexico because of its proximity to the United States. ... NAFTA [the North American Free Trade Agreement, which removed trade barriers between Mexico, the United States and Canada] got everybody excited about the possibilities. I think everyone made their initial ventures there, or had it on their books to begin in 1995, but once the devaluation of the Mexican peso began, many of them pulled back."[30]

C. Stewart Gentsch, president and general manager of Stanley Tools Worldwide, noted that the U.S.-style home centers are astoundingly popular wherever they open.

"A good example is Mexico. It was only a couple of years ago that the first home centers were planned for Mexico City. Before that, people would basically call a tradesman to fix something in the house or put in a lock or a closet organizer. Rarely would they go out and buy it themselves. If you were a tradesman, you would go to either a hardware store or a very focused store that might have only lock sets, or some other kind of single product. It would be in kind of a seedy neighborhood, and it would not be the kind of place where you would want to browse. In many

Stanley's new Home Decor Division offers decorative mirrors, closet storage products, closet doors and other products for the home.

cases, you would go to the counter and tell the guy what you want, and if you weren't specific, he would throw you out of the store.

"Then these home centers began to be planned for Mexico City. I asked local people whether or not they were going to be successful, and they said, 'They are going to be a failure because people don't buy these products themselves.'

"Even so, the first home center was built, probably about 50,000 or 60,000 square feet, with more than 100 feet of Stanley tools and Stanley hardware. Stanley had a whole wall presentation, as good a presentation as you would find in

any home center in the United States. I think it was the second or third day that they were open, when an American fellow that was responsible for the store called me in desperation and said, 'Everything is absolutely gone. I don't know what you can do to get me back in stock, but if I go through the system, it will take three or four days.' They opened on a Thursday, and on Saturday night, when they closed the store, the place was absolutely clean.

"It turned out that lots of people went into these stores and saw all the things they could have in their homes. In some cases, they bought them and bought the tools and did the installation. In other cases, they called their local tradesman for the installation. But it was more successful than anybody ever dreamed."[31]

Ayers recognizes Stanley's international potential, and in 1994, he stated his intention to increase international sales from 30 percent of total revenues to 40 percent, as noted in a *Hartford Courant* article.

"There is no stated time-line for the 40 percent goal, but Ayers calls the stakes crucial. Analysts agree, for reasons of simple arithmetic. Stanley, already a domestic market leader in several lines, cannot rely on 3 percent a year expansion of the economy — or worse — to increase revenues at a healthy rate. ... Ayers and other Stanley executives cite two chief reasons why the company has stepped up its off-shore moves. First, the company faces growing competitors in every region as markets open and tariffs decline. Second, customers such as Wal-Mart, Home Depot and Makro in Europe are becoming more international themselves. 'We can't have a major customer run off and not be with Stanley,' Ayers said."[32]

R. Alan Hunter, president and chief operating officer of The Stanley Works, standing, and Richard Ayers, chairman and chief executive officer.

At the 1994 annual meeting, Ayers again emphasized the importance of Stanley's international operations. "Global reach is important, not only because we can sell to more customers, but also because most economists predict that markets in Latin America and throughout Asia will grow 50 to 100 percent faster than the U.S. and Western Europe," he said.[33]

Four by Four

As the marketplace grows more aggressive, there is less tolerance for underperformers, Ayers said. "Anytime somebody believes there's a lot more potential at Stanley than we are achieving, we are at risk of being taken over. It's our performance, and how that performance is recognized in the marketplace, that counts. If we are performing well and are appropriately valued in the stock market, it would be too expensive for people to take us over."[34]

The centerpiece of this new, more aggressive strategy is the *Four by Four* program, announced in July 1995, which calls for growing the company to $4 billion in four years, and saving $400 million by reducing operating costs by $150 million and reducing assets by $250 million.

Stanley stock climbed $2.50 when the plan was announced July 19, 1995, reported the *Hartford Courant*. "The financial community hailed Stanley's move as a sign that the company, which posted record earnings last year, is serious about making hard choices to grow and remain profitable," the article noted.[35]

For the previous four years, the stock had been fluctuating between $36 and $40, said Patricia McLean, manager of corporate communications. But by September it had climbed to 46⅝.[36]

Ayers noted that Wall Street has traditionally underappreciated Stanley, despite the company's strong record of growth.

"They have a very short time horizon, and we went through a few flat years in terms of our performance. There was the trouble with Newell, and there were a couple of other issues that troubled us after that. I guess I can't be too critical of the investment community for losing interest in Stanley during that period of time. A lot of what we're doing right now is to rekindle that interest in the company by reminding them that there are a lot of good things that are present here at Stanley, and also clearly communicating that there is a lot of upside potential at Stanley."[37]

Hunter said the positive reaction from Wall Street is based on Stanley's longstanding reputation for quality and credibility.

"They needed to really believe that it was the right thing to do, and they needed to believe we could deliver. Now, if they believed both things 100 percent, I think the stock price would be a lot higher than it is today. So, from the investment community perspective, there are still some folks from Missouri, and we need to show them."[38]

To achieve this ambitious goal, the company must grow the business 10 percent a year regardless of the economy, while dramatically streamlining operations. A key component of the plan is the company's continuing strategy of growth through acquisition, Ayers said.

"We like to find businesses that have a leadership position, that have been well run and are performing well. We would like to have businesses that have good management that would stay with us when that business becomes part of Stanley. And I guess the final criteria that we consider, although some people would say that it ought to be first rather than last, is that we want

R. Alan Hunter (standing, center) and Richard Ayers (seated, right) enjoy a break for tea during a 1989 visit to Stanley operations in Japan.

to make sure that something we acquire is going to make a contribution to Stanley's shareholders at some point in time, and not just leave all the results or profits with the former owners through the high purchase price of the business."[39]

All the division presidents are eager to make the *Four by Four* goal a reality. Hunter noted that the program gives the presidents the opportunity to act on some of their more aggressive ideas.

"There's constant quarterly pressure in this country, if you're listed on the stock exchange. And because of that pressure, there are some things that maybe we should have done that we haven't. This program has taken the wraps off, giving people the ability to act on some things they probably know they should have done, but were not able to do, because of the pressure to earn each quarter."[40]

As part of the company's commitment to the program, The Stanley Works created the position of vice president of Strategy and Development, and hired Paul W. Russo to fill it. Russo was formerly co-chairman and co-CEO of SV Corporation, a Massachusetts-based international manufacturer of industrial valves. He graduated from the University of California at Berkeley and the Harvard School of Business Administration. "Paul Russo has an impressive work and educational background that is perfectly suited to our needs," Ayers said.[41]

The Stanley Works has no plans to diversify into unfamiliar areas. "Don't look for Stanley to be in the hotel business or to try the manufacture of personal computers," Ayers said, adding that the company's plans for diversification call for taking advantage of the customers and knowledge it already has.[42]

Ayers also explained some of the cost-cutting and asset-reduction measures of the *Four by Four* plan.

"We would like to take $150 million out of our cost structure, hopefully putting about half of that in our pocket and using the other half to be more aggressive in the market place, more active in advertising and product development. Maybe some tougher pricing, all to be more competitive. Then we are trying to reposition about $250 million of assets, where we believe we are underutilizing some investments that are on our balance sheet. That would include inventory, plants and equipment, maybe some vacant facilities that are still on our books. The total adds up to $400 million."[43]

Ayers pointed out that total Stanley spending is $2.3 billion annually, so he believes cutting expenses by $150 million is "very doable." With about $1.7 billion in assets, the company goal of cutting $250 million is also realistic, he said.[44]

A product or group that is not doing well and has poor prospects might be divested, even if it has done well in the past, he said. "We really have all of The Stanley Works under the magnifying glass from that perspective. ... Those things that are not contributing have to be taken out of the product line, and we will redeploy those assets and resources into things that will contribute to the company's future. We're doing that very aggressively right now."[45]

No division is safe from this sort of scrutiny, Ayers

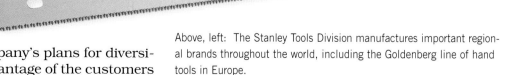

Above, left: The Stanley Tools Division manufactures important regional brands throughout the world, including the Goldenberg line of hand tools in Europe.

Above: This Jet-Cut saw was manufactured in France.

Stanley's legendary dedication to quality and customer service has helped it develop a reputation as the best tool manufacturer in the world.

said. "We are not wedded to any particular product category that might have been part of Stanley's history from the very beginning. We really have to be very, very critical about whether what we have is going to deliver for Stanley's future."[46]

In October 1995, The Stanley Works announced plans to eliminate 800 jobs, including 80 in Connecticut, and close four factories — a tool factory in Worcester, Massachusetts; a shoe repair equipment manufacturer in Atlanta; a fastening systems factory in Rancho Cucamonga, California; and a closet-organizer plant in France. Each plant employed about 100 people.[47]

Distribution centers in Kansas, Virginia and North Carolina are being eliminated, and the company's distribution system will be consolidated into a new distribution center in Charlotte, North Carolina. The Stanley Customer Support Division, established in 1994, will provide a single location for orders and customer service. Additional benefits were realized as part of an assessment of individual business segment performance and potential.

Ayers noted that cost reductions are only the beginning of a plan that will create a solid foundation for long-term growth for Stanley.

New Britain, Connecticut, is 119 miles from New York City.

It only seems farther than that.

People here live in the same houses their parents lived in.

Worship in churches where their grandparents worshipped.

And work for the company their great-grandfathers built. The Stanley Works.

So it's not surprising Stanley tools are made to last.

It would only be surprising if they weren't.

(MUSIC FADES OUT)

"There will be additional restructuring changes as we continue to focus on building a high-performance company," he said. "As we progress with our plans, the focus will move toward growth and expansion, rather than realignment and restructuring."[48]

CFO Huck praised Ayers for making Stanley a better, more competitive company.

"He had this vision of what Stanley could be, and he basically set out to build the foundation and put the infrastructure in place and figure out what the stress points were. ... I think many people would agree that some of the things that we have done here recently would not have been possible 10 years ago, and especially not in the time frame outlined today."[49]

Stanley Pride

For more than 150 years, Stanley has earned a reputation as a good corporate citizen and an excellent place to work. Every employee contributes to the Stanley reputation by providing excellent products and attentive customer service.

While each division sells individual products, The Stanley Works as a whole promotes the excellent image and reputation of the company. Television advertisements, such as the "New Britain" spots from 1989 highlighted Stanley's longstanding role in the community, said Donna Alexander, manager of marketing communications. "We sell an image of the company," she said. "The people and the spirit of the company."[50]

"Stanley's philosophy has been to have the best products and outstanding customer support, which yields a reputation and a name that people remember," said Patricia McLean, manager of corporate communications. "One of the responsibilities of the corporation to our different business units was to make sure that our name was kept in front of our customers. When

Stanley's 1989 "New Britain" commercials promoted the company's long history without emphasizing specific products.

we made an acquisition like Bostitch or Monarch, the Stanley name was there too. That's the general logic for producing the New Britain ads and some of the other ads."[51]

She said this philosophy continues into co-op advertising, in which both Stanley and a retailer share the costs of a promotional campaign.

"If you take a look at our co-op advertising today, you are going to see all of the different products that we sell. That was not the way it was done a few years ago. It was individual business units with individual products. Television and print ads are also coordinated to support the entire company."[52]

The Stanley image was not concocted for television commercials. It is a real sense of history, pride and community, as expressed by countless Stanley executives. "We hear it time and time again," said CFO Huck.

"This idea of something called Stanley that you can look back 150 years, and people associate it with quality tools, workmanship, reputation, trust and value. I think people who are closely connected to the company realize there are so many things here of great value. Long-term performance is one of them. But I think there is also incredible value in the wonderful heritage of the company, the strength of the name, the outstanding support we bring to the community, and the really special qualities of the Stanley people."[53]

"I characterize it as a family-oriented company," Gentsch said. "A company that is concerned about its employees, that makes honest, wholesome, high-quality products that people are proud of. Products that are used to build people's dreams, to construct things that please people. Products that are something to be proud of."[54]

President Hunter noted that it is the community of nearly 20,000 Stanley people that sets the company apart. Stanley employees are scattered around the globe, with about 30 percent outside the United States. Also playing an important role in the Stanley family are the collectors who cherish their tools and spend countless hours searching for new ones and researching the history of the ones they own.

"What makes Stanley different and successful over 153 years is its people, plain and simple. The tremendous vitality and devotion of its people. And that doesn't happen in a year or two years, and in fact it is not easy to maintain over 153 years. So obviously, the company and each of the leaders of the company and each of the businesses of the company has spent time on this. It's an important part of what we do, as intangible as it may seem."[55]

Ayers said he has worked to involve each and every Stanley employee in the ongoing process of making Stanley a successful company. "I think the story of Stanley is that it is an organization where everyone contributes."[56]

Posters, advertisements and catalogs are valuable collectors items. This poster is part of a series that appeared in the early twentieth century. (John Walter photograph/John Walter collection.)

COLLECTING STANLEY TOOLS

"Many collectors came to New Britain, home of Stanley, with the awe and reverence of pilgrims going to Mecca."

— New Britain Herald, 1993[1]

ANTIQUE STANLEY TOOLS have become valuable collectors items in recent years. Interest has intensified since the early seventies, but many collectors have been acquiring Stanley tools for decades, amassing collections that are worth tens of thousands of dollars. Stanley expert John Walter estimates that there are perhaps 20,000 tool collectors in the nation, with maybe 10 percent to 30 percent belonging to a tool-collecting club or organization.[2]

Antique tools hold a unique lure because they still perform the basic duty of a tool, which is to function as an extension of the human hand. A 100-year-old carpenter's rule still measures accurately today. A Defiance block plane from 1880 still makes wood smooth. Bill Harper, a Santa Fe cabinetmaker and furniture builder, explained why he collects antique tools in a 1991 *Smithsonian* magazine cover story, called "When Rules and Drills Drive You Just Plane Screwy," about antique tool collectors in America. "You take one of these old Stanley tools, and it feels *just right*," he said. "They made the handle of rosewood and it fits your hand just as if it was made for you specifically."[3]

"Harper picks up a Stanley 35 smoothing plane with a wooden body and says, 'This, I don't even use, because it's in such excellent con-

dition. I don't want to ding up the bottom any more than it is. You can take a shaving of one sixty-fourth of an inch off with this. I keep it around because it's an example of a beautiful old tool you'll just never see again.'

"But there is another reason Harper keeps these old relics of the anachronistic vocation he has assumed. 'I'm particular about the work that I put out,' he says. 'To me there's something about the quality of the tools I use. I feel an obligation to use a tool in the manner for which it was designed. You can picture in your mind the shop where they made these tools and the craftsmen who made them; and you can picture how they would want you to use it, keep it clean and sharp. Sometimes you feel as if you are working with the ghosts of your predecessors who worked before you.'"[4]

Stanley tools are particularly valued by collectors because of their superior quality and because of the company's long history. The Stanley Works is

Above: As The Stanley Works grew and diversified, it never abandoned its original product, hinges. This hanging hinge display is dated November 13, 1919. (Walter Jacob photograph/Charles and Walter Jacob collection.)

Division and collectors since 1984. When he started, Stoutenberg was amazed at the number of collectors brimming with questions about Stanley's history and products.

"There were letters and phone calls, saying, 'I found some old tool. How old is it? What is it? What is it worth? What was it used for?' ... Nobody thought too much about the job, because it was a minor detail, but they didn't realize the magnitude of the number of questions coming in. I volunteered to answer those questions. Out of necessity, that prompted me to be even more curious, so I could answer the questions. I don't have an official title, but I self-proclaim to be the historian. I answer historical questions. They're mostly tool-related, but also a little bit of the company's history as well."[12]

Tool collectors seek out others who share their passion, so it's not surprising that several organizations and conventions have been established. The Midwest Tool Collectors Association, considered the largest in the nation, even publishes its own magazine, *The Gristmill.* Tool auctions are also growing in popularity, said Walter Jacob.

Walter Jacob, and his twin brother, Charles, are the proud owners of one of the largest collections of Stanley tools in the world, believed to be worth millions of dollars. Besides sharing a passion for Stanley tools, the brothers are in business together and even seem to finish each other's sentences. They are cabinetmakers by trade, specializing in the conservation of antique furniture. They devote most of their spare time to the ardent pursuit of new tools for their cherished museum-quality collection.

The brothers now have so many tools that rounding out their collection has become something of an art form. They study the catalogs to make sure they don't waste their time at an auction that is offering items they already own.

"There are catalog sales up in Nashua, New Hampshire, and they have a summer flea market which is nothing but tools, and then various sales between that," Walter Jacob explained. "There's one auctioneer [in Pennsylvania] who has a giant tool auction about once a month. Or he might skip it every once in a while, depending on how many tools he has."[13]

Stanley tools typically comprise at least half of the items on the block at these auctions, said Charles Jacob. "A recent auction in Indianapolis was almost 75 percent Stanley."[14]

The brothers have recently begun cataloging their treasures using a computer program that lists its condition, value and unique qualities. Among their most valued items are a bronze Bailey scraper manufactured in 1855, and an original Bailey display case etched with the words "Bailey Patent Tools."

"Our favorites are Miller patents," Charles Jacob said. "Just a beautiful design. A beautiful

Above: Miller's Patent Plow Planes are popular collectors' items. (John Walter photograph/John Walter collection.)

Left: A rare No. 164 low angle plane, manufactured between 1926 and 1943, currently valued by collectors at $3,500. (John Walter photograph/John Walter collection.)

plane."[15] Miller's planes, manufactured between 1870 and 1897, are made of cast iron or gunmetal, and feature an ornate design and rosewood handle. Certain types sell for as much as $3,500.[16] John Walter, and his wife, Randa, wrote about the history and unique characteristics of Charles Miller's 1872 patent plow plane in the summer 1995 issue of *Stanley Tool Collectors News*. The article is illustrated with a photograph donated by Walter Jacob.

A meter–diagram patented by Augustus and Timothy Stanley in 1876. (Walter Jacob photograph/Charles and Walter Jacob collection.)

"Charles Miller's ornately stylized iron handle was a distinctive, identifying feature on all of his planes patented during the years between 1872 and 1876. This unique characteristic raises the question of whether any of Miller's designs were manufactured by anyone but him."[17]

by Stanley Works executives and guest speakers, a Collectors Banquet, a tour of Stanley's facility, and a barbecue on the Stanley grounds, hosted by the company.[20] More than 500 collectors from 40 states, Vancouver, Canada, and England participated, and *the New Britain Herald* reported that enthusiasm was high.

"According to [John] Walter, many collectors came to New Britain, home of Stanley, with the awe and reverence of pilgrims going to Mecca. One collector was so pumped up thinking about the visit, Walter said, that his voice trembled and his body shook."[21]

The Jacob brothers noted one negative aspect of the recent popularity of collecting antique tools. "As you get more and more tool collectors, it reduces the possibility of really getting a good collection," Walter Jacob said. "There are only so many antique tools out there. Like any collection, the people who were into it first have a better chance of having a more complete set because they were able to find it before it got so popular and so expensive."[18]

"It used to be that every Sunday morning, I would go to the antique flea markets and find a lot of good stuff there," added Charles Jacob. "Now I can go up there Sunday after Sunday and not find anything."[19]

In honor of Stanley's 150th anniversary in 1993, John Walter organized the Stanley Tool Collector's Convention in New Britain. The convention lasted three days and featured appearances

For more information on old Stanley tools, *Stanley Tool Collector News*, and books on Stanley, contact John Walter, C\O The Old Tool Shop, 208 Front Street, Marietta, Ohio, 45750.

Commemorative toys like this often become valuable to collectors. This truck was manufactured by Corgi in the 1980s. (John Walter photograph/John Walter collection.)

NOTES TO SOURCES

Chapter One

1. *Proud of Our Past. 150 Years of Growth through Excellence at The Stanley Works*, booklet published by The Stanley Works, New Britain, Connecticut, 1993, inside cover.
2. Robert Keith Leavitt, *Foundations for the Future. The History of The Stanley Works*, privately published in New Britain, Connecticut, for The Stanley Works, 1951, p. 8.
3. *Ibid.*, p. 42. Originally from Odell Shepard, Peddler's Progress, *The Life of Bronson Alcott* (Boston, Massachusetts: Little, Brown and Company, 1939.)
4. Leavitt, p. 10.
5. *Ibid.*, p. 8.
6. *Proud of Our Past*, p. 5.
7. *The Stanley Families of America*, privately published in 1887, p. 69.
8. "Ex–Mayor Stanley — Incidents of His Life that May be Read with Interest," *New Britain Herald*, August 10, 1883.
9. Leavitt, p. 9.
10. *Ibid.*
11. *Ibid.*
12. *Ibid.*
13. David N. Camp, *History of New Britain*. (New Britain, Connecticut: W.B. Thomson and Company, 1889), p. 481.
14. Leavitt, p. 11.
15. *New Britain Herald*, August 10, 1883.
16. Leavitt, p. 12.
17. *Ibid.*
18. *Ibid.*
19. *Ibid.*, p. 13.
20. *Ibid.*
21. Camp, p. 481.
22. Leavitt, p. 17.
23. *Ibid.*
24. Camp, p. 168.
25. *Ibid.*, p. 482.
26. Leavitt, p. 19.
27. Camp, as quoted in Leavitt, p. 20.
28. *Proud of Our Past*, p. 1.
29. Leavitt, p. 20.
30. *Ibid.*
31. *New Britain Herald*, August 10, 1883.
32. "Changes at The Stanley Works," *Hardware Age* magazine, New York, March 4, 1915.
33. Leavitt, p. 22.
34. *Ibid.*, p. 23.
35. *Ibid.*
36. *Ibid.*
37. *Ibid.*, p. 24.
38. *Ibid.*
39. *Ibid.*

Chapter Two

1. Robert Keith Leavitt, *Foundations for the Future. The History of The Stanley Works*, privately published in New Britain, Connecticut, for The Stanley Works, 1951, p. 36.
2. *Ibid.*
3. *Ibid.*, p. 25.
4. Roy F. Soule, "William H. Hart," *Hardware Age* magazine, New York, February 28, 1918.
5. Leavitt, p. 26.
6. *Ibid.*
7. Soule article.
8. Leavitt, p. 26.
9. Lillian Hart Tryon, *A Biographical and Historical Sketch of William H. Hart, 1834-1919*, privately published in New Britain, Connecticut, for The Stanley Works, 1929. This book has no page numbers.
10. Leavitt, p. 27.
11. *Ibid.*
12. *Ibid.*, p. 28.
13. Letter from William Hart to his son, Walter, July 8, 1919.
14. Soule article.
15. Tryon book.
16. Leavitt, p. 28.
17. *Biography of William Hart*, written by his son Walter, privately published October 23, 1919.
18. Soule article.
19. William Hart biography.
20. "Changes at The Stanley Works," *Hardware Age* magazine, New York, March 4, 1915.
21. William Hart biography.
22. Leavitt, p. 36.
23. *Proud of Our Past. 150 Years of Growth through Excellence at The Stanley Works*, booklet published by The Stanley Works, New Britain, Connecticut, 1993, p. 7.
24. Soule article.
25. Tryon book.
26. *Ibid.*
27. Letter from Frederick T. Stanley to Capt. V.B. Chamberlain, dated September 15, 1862.
28. Letter from Frederick T. Stanley to Capt. V.B. Chamberlain, dated December 24, 1861.
29. Leavitt, p. 36.
30. *Ibid.*
31. *Ibid.*
32. 1915 *Hardware Age* article.
33. Leavitt, p. 38.

34. 1915 *Hardware Age* article.
35. Leavitt, p. 43.
36. *Ibid.*
37. *Ibid.*, p. 42.
38. Letter from William Hart to his son Walter, dated June 23, 1919.
39. *Ibid.*
40. Leavitt, p. 43.
41. 1915 *Hardware Age* article.
42. *Ibid.*

Chapter Three

1. Roy F. Soule, "William H. Hart," *Hardware Age* magazine, New York, February 28, 1918.
2. *Ibid.*
3. "Changes at The Stanley Works," *Hardware Age* magazine, New York, March 4, 1915.
4. *Ibid.*
5. Robert Keith Leavitt, *Foundations for the Future. The History of The Stanley Works*, privately published in New Britain, Connecticut, for The Stanley Works, 1951, p. 47.
6. *Ibid.*, p. 46.
7. *Ibid.*, p. 48.
8. Soule article.
9. Leavitt, p. 48.
10. Lillian Hart Tryon, *A Biographical and Historical Sketch of William H. Hart, 1834-1919*, privately published in New Britain, Connecticut, for The Stanley Works, 1929. This book has no page numbers.
11. Soule article.
12. Leavitt, p. 48.
13. Tryon, end of Chapter Five.
14. *Ibid.*
15. 1915 *Hardware Age* article.
16. Leavitt, p. 45.
17. Soule article.
18. *Ibid.*
19. *Biography of William Hart*, written by his son, Walter, published October 23, 1919.
20. Leavitt, p. 50.
21. *Ibid.*
22. *Ibid.*
23. Tryon book.
24. Leavitt, p. 51.
25. *Ibid.*
26. Copy of the certificate, 1876.
27. Leavitt, p. 51.
28. *Ibid.*, p. 52.
29. *Ibid.*
30. *Proud of Our Past*, p. 1.
31. Leavitt, p. 55.

32. *Ibid.*
33. Soule article.
34. *Proud of Our Past,* p. 7.
35. Leavitt, pp. 53-54.
36. Tryon book.
37. *Ibid.*
38. Leavitt, p. 59.
39. *Ibid.,* pp. 59-60.
40. *Ibid.,* p. 61.
41. *Ibid.*
42. *Ibid.*
43. *Ibid.,* p. 63.
44. "Obituary of Hon. F.T. Stanley," *New Britain Herald,* August 4, 1883.
45. *Ibid.*
46. David N. Camp, *History of New Britain.* (New Britain, Connecticut: W.B. Thomson and Company, 1889), p. 191.

Chapter Four

1. Roy F. Soule, "William H. Hart," *Hardware Age* magazine, New York, February 28, 1918.
2. Robert Keith Leavitt, *Foundations for the Future. The History of The Stanley Works,* privately published in New Britain, Connecticut, for The Stanley Works, 1951, p. 64.
3. *Ibid.,* pp. 64-65.
4. John Sloan, "Making Boxwood Rules in Earlier Days," *The Stanley World,* March 1938, p. 11.
5. Leavitt, p. 65.
6. *Ibid.,* p. 70.
7. *Ibid.*
8. Ethelbert Allen Moore, *Four Decades with The Stanley Works, 1889-1929,* privately published in New Britain, Connecticut, 1950, p. 10.
9. Leavitt, p. 66.
10. *Ibid,* p. 67.
11. *Ibid.,* p. 68.
12. *The Autobiography of S. Corrugated Hinge,* published in 1900 by The Stanley Works, New Britain, Connecticut.
13. Roy F. Soule, "William H. Hart," *Hardware Age* magazine, New York, February 28, 1918.
14. Moore, p. 10.
15. *Ibid.,* p. 7.
16. Soule article.
17. *Ibid.*
18. "Former S.W. Head is Dead, Aged 90," *New Britain Herald,* July 14, 1951.
19. Leavitt, p. 69.
20. *Ibid.,* p. 71.
21. *Ibid.*
22. *Ibid.,* p. 75.
23. "Changes at The Stanley Works," *Hardware Age* magazine, New York, March 4, 1915.

24. Leavitt, p. 73.
25. Moore, p. 33.
26. *Ibid.,* pp. 33-34.
27. Leavitt, p. 88.
28. *Ibid.,* p. 93.
29. *Ibid.,* p. 93.
30. *Ibid.,* p. 89.
31. *Ibid.,* p. 90.
32. *Ibid.,* pp. 89-90.
33. Moore, p. 16.
34. *Ibid.,* pp. 53-54.

Chapter Five

1. "Changes at The Stanley Works," *Hardware Age* magazine, New York, March 4, 1915.
2. Ethelbert Allen Moore, *Four Decades with The Stanley Works, 1889-1929,* privately published in New Britain, Connecticut, 1950, p. 34.
3. Biography of William Hart, written by his son Walter, published October 23, 1919.
4. Hoyt Pease, interviewed by the author, New Britain, Connecticut, March 20, 1995. Transcript, p. 2.
5. Robert Keith Leavitt, *Foundations for the Future. The History of The Stanley Works,* privately published in New Britain, Connecticut, for The Stanley Works, 1951, p. 87.
6. Moore, p. 63.
7. Leavitt, p. 91.
8. *Ibid.*
9. *Ibid.,* p. 92.
10. Letter from William Hart to his son Walter, 1919.
11. Moore, p. 54.
12. *Ibid.,* pp. 55-56.
13. *Ibid.,* p. 56.
14. Leavitt, p. 89.
15. Moore, p. 17.
16. *Ibid.*
17. Leavitt, p. 95.
18. *Ibid.*
19. Moore, p. 21.
20. *Ibid.*
21. 1915 *Hardware Age* article.
22. Moore, p. 66.
23. *Ibid.,* pp. 70-71.
24. Leavitt, pp. 97-98.
25. *Ibid.,* p. 98.
26. *Ibid.,* p. 97.
27. *The Stanley Workers,* March 7, 1918, p. 7.
28. *The Stanley Workers,* January 24, 1918, p. 4.
29. Roy F. Soule, "William H. Hart," *Hardware Age* magazine, New York, February 28, 1918.
30. *Ibid.*
31. Leavitt, p. 100.
32. *Ibid.,* p. 99.

33. *The Hartford Courant,* December 14, 1919.
34. Leavitt, p. 102.
35. *Ibid.*

Chapter Six

1. *Tool Traditions,* a catalog published in 1995 by The Stanley Works, p. 3.
2. Charles Jacob and Walter Jacob, notes to author, December 1995.
3. *Ibid.*
4. Robert Keith Leavitt, *Foundations for the Future. The History of The Stanley Works,* privately published in New Britain, Connecticut, for The Stanley Works, 1951, p. 32.
5. Phil Stanley, *Boxwood & Ivory Stanley Traditional Rules,* 1855-1975, published in Westborough, Massachusetts by The Stanley Works Publishing Company, 1984, p. 8.
6. Leavitt, p. 33.
7. *Ibid.*
8. *Ibid.*
9. *Ibid.,* p. 34.
10. Speech by Fred Curry at the Midwest Tool Collectors Association Meeting, Memphis, Tennessee, October 10, 1980.
11. Leavitt, p. 34.
12. *Ibid.,* p. 76.
13. John Walter, *Antique and Collectible Stanley Tools,* published by the Tool Merchant, Marietta, Ohio, 1990, p. 294.
14. "Do You Know These Facts about Boxwood?" 1938 article, reprinted in *Stanley Tool Collector News,* Volume 6, Number 14, Spring 1995, p. 32.
15. *Ibid.,* p. 32.
16. Carl Stoutenberg, notes to author, December 5, 1995.
17. Carl Stoutenberg, interviewed by the author, March 20, 1995, New Britain, Connecticut. Transcript, p. 8.
18. Leavitt, p. 78.
19. Alvin Sellens, *The Stanley Plane -- A History and Descriptive Inventory,* published in South Burlington, Vermont, by The Early American Industries Association, 1975, p. 22.
20. Leavitt, p. 79.
21. *Ibid.*
22. *Ibid.*
23. Carl Stoutenberg, notes to author, December 5, 1995.
24. *Ibid.*
25. *Tool Traditions,* p. 3.
26. Leavitt, p. 80.
27. *Ibid.*
28. *Ibid.,* p. 81.
29. Arthur E. McEvoy, "The Old Rule Shop will Become History," *New Britain Herald,*

December 27, 1963.

30. Leavitt, p. 82.

31. *Ibid.*, p. 80.

32. *Ibid.*, p. 84.

33. *Ibid.*, pp. 85-86.

34. *Ibid.*

35. *Ibid.*, p. 109.

36. *Ibid.*, p. 83.

37. *Ibid.*, p. 112.

38. Minutes of the Operations Committee, July 15, 1917.

39. Memo from A.S. Duncan to M.A. Coe, Superintendent, October 6, 1926.

40. Letter to Employees, January 8, 1914.

41. Minutes of the Operations Committee, June 2, 1916.

42. Leavitt, p. 107.

43. *Ibid.*, p. 108.

44. *Ibid.*

45. *Ibid.*

46. *Ibid.*

47. *Ibid.*

48. Francis Zambrello, interviewed by Torrey Kim, South Shaftsbury, Vermont, April 28, 1995. Transcript, p. 2.

49. *Ibid.*, p. 11.

50. *Ibid.*, p. 2.

51. *Ibid.*, p. 4.

52. Letter from Superintendent H.J. Cook to all Stanley Rule & Level Employees, January 4, 1918.

53. Minutes of the Operations Committee, October 22, 1918 and November 7, 1918.

54. Leavitt, p. 113.

55. *Ibid.*

Chapter Seven

1. Announcement booklet produced by E.A. Moore, dated May 1, 1920.

2. Ethelbert Allen Moore, *Four Decades with The Stanley Works, 1889-1929*, privately published in New Britain, Connecticut, 1950, p. 78.

3. Robert Keith Leavitt, *Foundations for the Future. The History of The Stanley Works*, privately published in New Britain, Connecticut, for The Stanley Works, 1951, p. 82.

4. Moore, p. 79.

5. *Ibid.*, pp. 80-81.

6. Announcement booklet.

7. Leavitt, p. 117.

8. *Ibid.*

9. Phil Stanley, *Boxwood & Ivory Stanley Traditional Rules*, 1855-1975, published in Westborough, Massachusetts by The Stanley Works Publishing Company, 1984, p. 12.

10. *Ibid.*

11. Leavitt, p. 120.

12. *The Stanley Workers*, March 4, 1921.

13. Hoyt C. Pease, interviewed by the author, March 20, 1995, New Britain, Connecticut. Transcript, p. 4.

14. *Defiance by Stanley*, a pamphlet produced by Stanley Tools.

15. "$1,000,000 Power Plant Replaces Farmington River Water Wheels," *Hartford Daily Times*, October 24, 1925.

16. Moore, p. 22.

17. Leavitt, p. 123.

18. *Ibid.*, p. 124.

19. *Ibid.*, p. 125.

20. *Ibid.*

21. *Ibid.*

22. *Ibid.*, p. 134.

23. Moore, pp. 102-106.

24. Edward C. Pritchard, *Richard E. Pritchard, A Man of Industry*, privately published in 1988, p. 15.

25. *Ibid.*, p. 24.

26. *Ibid.*

27. *Ibid.*

28. Leavitt, p. 129.

29. *Ibid.*, p. 130.

30. *Ibid.*

31. *Ibid.*

32. 1929, published by The Stanley Works, p. 7.

33. 1930 Annual Report, published by The Stanley Works, p. 7.

34. Leavitt, p. 132.

35. *Ibid.*

36. Jack R. Ryan, "Push Door? Pull? It's Neither Now," *The New York Times*, December 20, 1955.

37. Carl Stoutenberg, notes to author, December 5, 1995.

38. *Ibid.*

39. Phil Stanley book, p. 14.

40. *Ibid.*

Chapter Eight

1. Edward C. Pritchard, *Richard E. Pritchard, A Man of Industry*, privately published in 1988, p. 36.

2. Robert Keith Leavitt, *Foundations for the Future. The History of The Stanley Works*, privately published in New Britain, Connecticut, for The Stanley Works, 1951, p. 134.

3. Hoyt C. Pease, interviewed by the author, March 20, 1995, New Britain, Connecticut. Transcript, p. 7.

4. Leavitt, p. 134.

5. *Ibid.*, p. 138.

6. Donald W. Davis, interviewed by the author, Hobe Sound, Florida, March 17, 1995.

Transcript, p. 21.

7. Leavitt, p. 135.

8. Ronald Gilrain, interviewed by the author, March 27, 1995, New Britain, Connecticut. Transcript, p. 16.

9. "S.W. War Slogan Chosen by Judges," *New Britain Herald*, July 9, 1942.

10. *Ibid.*

11. *The Stanley World*, July 11, 1941.

12. "Stanley Workers Receive "E" Award," *New Britain Herald*, January 20, 1943.

13. *Ibid.*, p. 139.

14. *Ibid.*

15. *Ibid.*, p. 140.

16. "Leaders of Industry Optimistic, Survey Made by C. of C. Shows; Employment Expected to Pick Up," *New Britain Herald*, August 24, 1945.

17. Leavitt, p. 140.

18. "Cairns President of Stanley Works in Officer Change," *New Britain Herald*, March 31, 1950.

19. Leavitt, p. 141.

20. *Ibid.*, p. 143.

21. *Ibid.*, p. 143.

22. Leavitt, p. *143*.

23. Tom Jones, interviewed by the author, October 2, 1995, New Britain, Connecticut. Transcript, p. 9.

24. Pease interview, pp. 8-9.

25. Pease interview, p. 1.

26. Leavitt, p. 142.

27. "S.W. Ruhr Factory Virtually Intact," *New Britain Herald*, June 5, 1945.

28. "New Britain Machine Buildings on Chestnut Street Bought by S.W. for Tools Division Occupancy," *New Britain Herald*, March 10, 1950.

29. *Ibid.*

30. John C. Cairns, "A Look at the 1950s," *Stanley World*, April 1960, p. 9.

31. 1966 Advertisement.

32. "A Look at the 1950s," p. 4.

33. 1951 Annual Report, published by The Stanley Works, p. 10.

34. "S.W. Buys out Small Concern in New Jersey," *New Britain Herald*, November 8, 1952.

35. Pritchard, p. 40.

36. *Ibid.*

37. "Stanley Works Buying Wallingford Concern," *The Hartford Times*, September 16, 1954.

38. "Stanley Works Ready to Enter Aluminum Field," *New Britain Herald*, November 4, 1955.

39. Cairns, p. 5.

40. "Do It Yourself, The New Billion-Dollar Hobby," *Time*, August 2, 1954.

41. 1953 Annual Report, published by The Stanley Works, p. 12.

42. 1956 Annual Report, published by The

Stanley Works, p. 8.

43. "Unexpected Retirement," *New Britain Herald*, April 1, 1955.

44. "E. Allen Moore Dies, Rose at Stanley Works from Clerk to Leader," *New Britain Herald*, February 13, 1956.

45. Cairns, p. 4.

46. "Government Runs SW Steel Plant," *New Britain Herald*, April 9, 1952.

47. "John C. Cairns, Our President," *The Stanley World*, April 1960, p. 7.

48. "Review of The Stanley Works," a special report from Putnam & Company, R.C. Hector, Hartford, Connecticut, June 2, 1961, p. 3.

49. *Ibid.*

50. "New $3 Million Steel Division At Stanley Works in Operation Employing Total of 343 People," *New Britain Herald*, January 10, 1955.

51. 1957 Annual Report, published by The Stanley Works, p. 3.

52. Cairns, p. 8.

53. "Stanley Installing 'Electronic Brain,'" *New Britain Herald*, August 13, 1956.

54. "SW Private Phone System Largest in City," *New Britain Herald*, November 22, 1955.

55. "110-Ton Machine Being Installed at Stanley Works," *New Britain Herald*, July 8, 1957.

56. Cairns, p. 6.

57. Cairns, p. 10.

58. 1957 Annual Report, p. 7.

Chapter Nine

1. "The Stanley Works," stock recommendation by Blyth & Company as of December 31, 1961. Published April, 1962.

2. Stanley advertisement in September 22, 1960 issue of *Hardware Age*, and September 1960 issue of *Hardware Retailer* and *Building Supply News*.

3. Press release, The Stanley Works, 1960.

4. Francis Zambrello, interviewed by Torrey Kim, South Shaftsbury, Vermont, April 28, 1995. Transcript, p. 3.

5. *Ibid.*, pp. 3-4.

6. Press Release, The Stanley Works, January 12, 1960.

7. Zambrello interview, p. 3.

8. "Stanley Works to Acquire Tool Company in London," *New Britain Herald*, November 30, 1961.

9. 1961 Annual Report, published by The Stanley Works, p. 6.

10. Blyth & Company stock recommendation.

11. "Stanley Works Designates New Executive Vice President Here," *New Britain Herald*, September 9, 1959.

12. Donald W. Davis, interviewed by the author,

Hobe Sound, Florida, March 17, 1995. Transcript, pp. 25-26.

13. Davis interview, pp. 23-24.

14. "Brought to Your Door," *Stanley News*, published by The Stanley Works, New Britain, Connecticut, April 1937, Front Cover.

15. Richard C. Hastings, interviewed by the author, March 20, 1995, New Britain, Connecticut. Transcript, p. 3.

16. Hoyt Pease, interviewed by the author, March 20, 1995, New Britain, Connecticut. Transcript, p. 25.

17. "Special Report from Putnam & Company," stock recommendation, Hartford, Connecticut, January 15, 1964, p. 4.

18. *Ibid.*

19. Donald Davis, interviewed by the author, March 17, 1995, Hobe Sound, Florida. Transcript, p. 30.

20. 1963 Annual Report, published by The Stanley Works, p. 4.

21. 1964 Annual Report, published by The Stanley Works, p. 4.

22. "Stanley-Titan Tie-Up Makes Hand Tool News," *Australian Hardware Journal*, June 1, 1963.

23. 1963 Annual Report, p. 6.

24. *Ibid.*

25. "Stanley Chemical Buys Norwood, Mass. Firm," *New Britain Herald*, February 7, 1964.

26. "Efficiency, Comfort Mark New Tools Plant," *New Britain Herald*, January 16, 1964.

27. "Stanley Works Plans Plant in Farmington," *Hartford Times*, January 9, 1967.

28. 1964 Annual Report, p. 3.

29. Press Release, The Stanley Works, April 29, 1965.

30. "SW in Agreement to Purchase Firm in Long Island, NY," *New Britain Herald*, January 3, 1966.

31. Press release, The Stanley Works, 1973.

32. "Don Davis -- Young Head for an Old Company," *Inside Story*, Winter 1967-1968, p. 31.

33. "Stanley Works International in Scope," *Hartford Courant*, June 15, 1969.

34. John Parsons, interviewed by the author, March 20, 1995, New Britain, Connecticut. Transcript, p. 15.

Chapter Ten

1. Donald W. Davis, interviewed by the author, Hobe Sound, Florida, March 28, 1995. Transcript, pp. 12-13.

2. "Stanley Works Elects Davis, Cairns Retiring," *Hartford Times*, April 28, 1966.

3. "Don Davis — Young Head for an Old Com-

pany," *Inside Story*, Winter 1967-1968, p. 30.

4. *Ibid.*

5. "Stanley Works is one of 400 Largest Corporations in the United States," *United States Investor*, August 14, 1967, p. 19.

6. Richard Huck, interviewed by the author, September 12, 1995, New Britain, Connecticut. Transcript, p. 40.

7. "Young Head for an Old Company," p. 31.

8. Davis interview, March 17, 1995, pp. 36-46.

9. 1967 Annual Report, published by The Stanley Works, p. 5.

10. Davis interview, March 28, 1995, pp. 12-13.

11. *Ibid.*, pp. 14-15.

12. 1974 Annual Report, published by The Stanley Works, p. 2.

13. "State Receives Museum Deed from Local Firm," by Anthony G. Grey, *New Britain Herald*, December 27, 1968.

14. "Sloane-Stanley Museum Interesting Spot to Visit," *New Britain Herald*, June 6, 1969.

15. Richard Joseph, "A Museum of Tools," *Philadelphia Inquirer*, September 21, 1969.

16. 1956 Annual Report, published by The Stanley Works, p. 4.

17. Richard C. Hastings, interviewed by the author, March 20, 1995. New Britain, Connecticut. Transcript, p. 21.

18. Ted Dempsey, "Kidnapper Gets $34,000 from Stanley Officials," *Hartford Times*, May 24, 1968.

19. 1970 Annual Report, published by *The Stanley Works*, pp. 6-8.

20. *Ibid.*, p. 1.

21. "Davis is Recipient of McAuliffe Medal," *New Britain Herald*, May 19, 1971.

22. 1970 Annual Report, p. 10.

23. *Ibid.*, p. 4.

24. 1971 Annual Report, published by The Stanley Works, p. 1.

25. 1975 Annual Report, published by The Stanley Works, p. 3.

26. 1972 Annual Report, p. 1.

27. 1973 Annual Report, published by The Stanley Works, p. 1.

28. *Ibid.*

29. Thomas P. Shiel, "SW Dedicates New Laboratory," *New Britain Herald*, January 11, 1974.

30. 1975 Annual Report, p. 2.

31. Huck interview, p. 4.

32. *Ibid.*

33. *Ibid.*, pp. 5-6.

34. "Stanley Works Gives Land to Nature Conservancy," *The Lakeview Journal*, Lakeview, Connecticut, October 7, 1976.

35. Dick Wolff, "The Miraculous Return," Field & Stream, April 1979.

36. "Connecticut Conference presents 'Samar-

itan Award,'" *A.D.*, March 1975, p. 59.

Chapter Eleven

1. 1993 Annual Report, published by The Stanley Works, p. 12.
2. Public Affairs Newsletter, Volume 2, Number 2, published by The Stanley Works, October 1976.
3. Donald W. Davis, speech upon receiving the 1986 National Humanitarian Award from the National Jewish Center for Immunology and Respiratory Medicine, March 10, 1986.
4. Public Affairs Newsletter, Volume 3, Number 1, published by The Stanley Works, May 1977.
5. Public Affairs Newsletter, Volume 3, Number 2, published by The Stanley Works, November 1977.
6. Public Affairs Newsletter, Volume 5, Number 1, published by The Stanley Works, February 1979.
7. Patricia McLean, interviewed by the author, New Britain, Connecticut, September 12, 1995. Transcript, p. 19.
8. 1993 Annual Report, p. 12.
9. Public Affairs Newsletter, Volume 8, Number 2, published by The Stanley Works, July 1982.
10. Public Affairs Newsletter, Volume 9, Number 2, published by The Stanley Works, April 1983.
11. Public Affairs Newsletter, Volume 11, Number 3, published by The Stanley Works, December 1985.
12. 1976 Annual Report, published by The Stanley Works, p. 4.
13. "Stanley Works Chief Heads up State Business Unit," *Business Review*, January 1977.
14. *Ibid.*
15. 1978 Annual Report, published by The Stanley Works, p. 1.
16. 1979 Annual Report, published by The Stanley Works, p. 1.
17. "Stanley Works: Capitalizing on the Homeowner Do-It-Yourself Trend," *Business Week*, February 26, 1979, p. 125.
18. *Ibid.*, p. 126.
19. *Business Week*, February 26, 1979, p. 126.
20. *Ibid.*
21. 1977 Annual Report, published by The Stanley Works, p. 15.
22. James V. Healion, "Trend Toward Doing it Yourself Creates Boon for Tool Company," *Springfield Daily News*, July 8, 1979.
23. 1978 Annual Report, p. 6.
24. 1977 Annual Report, p. 15.
25. *Ibid.*
26. *Ibid.*
27 "Do-It-Yourself, Growth Industry for the 80s," published by The Stanley Works, 1981.
28. 1980 Annual Report, published by The

Stanley Works, p. 2.
29. Stanley *Fact Book*, published by The Stanley Works, May 1981, p. 3.
30. *Ibid.*, p. 12.
31. *Fact Book*, p. 3.
32. *Ibid.*, p. 2.
33. Donald W. Davis, interviewed by the author, Hobe Sound, Florida, March 28, 1995. Transcript, pp. 27-28.
34. Thomas E. Mahoney, interviewed by the author, New Britain, Connecticut, September 11, 1995. Transcript, p. 14.
35. Ayers interview, pp. 46-47.
36. Ayers interview, p. 49.
37. 1980 Annual Report, p. 3.
38. Charles Blossom, interviewed by the author, October 9, 1995, by telephone. Transcript, p. 15.
39. *Ibid.*, p. 10.
40. Ayers interview, pp. 19-20.
41. *Ibid, 22-23.*
42. *Ibid.*
43. Sid DeBoer, "Head of SW Finds 'Time' to View Today's World", *New Britain Herald*, November 11, 1981.
44. *Ibid.*
45. *Ibid.*

Chapter Twelve

1. Timothy Heider, "Stanley to Build New Headquarters", *Hartford Courant*, August 8, 1981.
2. 1980 Annual Report, published by The Stanley Works, p. 3.
3. Donald W. Davis, interviewed by the author, Hobe Sound, Florida, March 28, 1995. Transcript, p. 20.
4. Article written by Richard H. Ayers, "Richard H. Ayers, President and Chief Operating Officer, The Stanley Works," *Hardware Merchandiser*, October 1986, p. 1.
5. *Ibid.*, p. 2.
6. R. Alan Hunter, interviewed by the author, September 29, 1995, by telephone. Transcript, p. 10.
7. Davis interview, March 17, 1995, Transcript, pp. 55-56.
8. Ayers article, *Hardware Merchandiser*, p. 4.
9. 1982 Annual Report, published by The Stanley Works, p. 24.
10. 1983 Annual Report, published by The Stanley Works, p. 1.
11. S. Avery Brown, "Stanley Works at Home in New Britain," *Hartford Courant*, August 8, 1981.
12. "Stanley to Build New Headquarters."
13. Ronald Gilrain, interviewed by the author, March 27, 1995, New Britain, Connecticut.

Transcript, pp. 14-15.
14. "SW Chairman Named NB 'Man of Year,'" *New Britain Herald*, January 7, 1984.
15. 1984 Annual Report, published by The Stanley Works, inside cover.
16. "The Stanley Works," stock recommendation by First Boston Research, July 18, 1985, p. 3.
17. Wayne King, interviewed by the author, October 10, 1995, New Britain, Connecticut. Transcript, p. 5.
18. First Boston Research stock recommendation, p. 11.
19. *Ibid.*, p. 40.
20. *Ibid.*
21. 1986 Annual Report, p. 2.
22. *Ibid*, p. 2.
23. John Turpin, interviewed by the author, October 9, 1995, by telephone. Transcript, p. 2.
24. 1986 Annual Report, pp. 2-3.
25. Ayers article, *Hardware Merchandiser.*
26. 1987 Annual Report, published by The Stanley Works, p. 1.
27. *Ibid.*, p. 6.
28. Joseph L. Jones, interviewed by the author, September 11, 1995, New Britain, Connecticut. Transcript, p. 6.
29. 1988 Annual Report, published by The Stanley Works, p. 3.
30. 1989 Annual Report, published by The Stanley Works, p. 13.

Chapter Thirteen

1. Richard H. Ayers, interviewed by the author, September 12, 1995, New Britain, Connecticut. Transcript, pp. 50-51.
2. Donald W. Davis, interviewed by the author, Hobe Sound, Florida, March 28, 1995. Transcript, p. 5.
3. "Celebration of Service," booklet honoring Donald W. Davis, published by The Stanley Works, 1989.
4. *Ibid.*
5. *Ibid.*
6. Ayers interview, p. 53.
7. 1988 Annual Report, published by The Stanley Works, p. 3.
8. *Ibid.*
9. 1989 Annual Report, p. 1.
10. 1990 Annual Report, p. 1.
11. 1991 Annual Report, p. 3.
12. *Ibid.*
13. Francis interview, p. 7.
14. Ayers interview, pp. 50-51.
15. Patricia McLean, interviewed by the author, New Britain, Connecticut, September 12,

1995. Transcript, p. 34.

16. Stewart Gentsch, interviewed by the author, September 11, 1995, New Britain, Connecticut. Transcript, p. 25.

17. Robert Hudson, interviewed by the author, October 9, 1995, New Britain, Connecticut. Transcript, p. 16.

18. Hudson interview, p. 12.

19. Gentsch interview, p. 10.

20. Joseph L. Jones, interviewed by the author, September 15, 1995, New Britain, Connecticut. Transcript, p. 3.

21. Hudson interview, p. 12.

22. John Francis, interviewed by the author, October 9, 1995, by telephone. Transcript, p. 3.

23. Richard Huck, interviewed by the author, September 12, 1995, New Britain, Connecticut. Transcript, pp. 7-9.

24. Carl Stoutenberg, interviewed by the author, March 20, 1995. New Britain, Connecticut. Transcript, pp. 12-13.

25. Ayers interview, pp. 28-31.

26. Letter from Richard H. Ayers to Fellow Employees, January 2, 1992.

27. Ayers interview, p. 32.

28. Ibid, p. 34.

29. Ayers interview, p. 35.

30. *Ibid.*, p. 33.

31. "'They Get to Go Away,'" editorial in the *New Britain Herald*, October 6, 1992.

32. 1992 Annual Report, p. 20.

33. Donna Alexander, interviewed by the author, September 11, 1995, New Britain, Connecticut. Transcript, p 8.

34. 1992 Annual Report, p. 1.

35. Alexander interview, p. 6.

36. *Ibid.*, p. 9.

37. *Ibid.*, p. 8.

Chapter Fourteen

1. "Proud of Our Past. 150 Years of Growth Through Excellence at The Stanley Works," published in 1993 by The Stanley Works, inside cover.

2. *Ibid.*

3. R. Alan Hunter, interviewed by the author, September 29, 1995, by telephone. Transcript, p. 4.

4. 1993 Annual Report, published by The Stanley Works, p. 32.

5. *Ibid.*, p. 25.

6. 1993 Annual Report, pp. 4-5.

7. Richard Huck, interviewed by the author, September 12, 1995, New Britain, Connecticut. Transcript, p. 13.

8. 1994 Annual Report, published by The Stanley Works, p. 26.

9. Dan Haar, "Stanley's World," *Hartford Courant*, June 19, 1995.

10. Joseph L. Jones interview, p. 20.

11. *Ibid.*

12. Gentsch interview, p. 22.

13. Charles Blossom, interviewed by the author, October 9, 1995, by telephone. Transcript, p. 8.

14. John Turpin, interviewed by the author, October 9, 1995, by telephone. Transcript, p. 4.

15. *Ibid.*, p. 6.

16. Henning Kornbrekke, interviewed by the author, September 12, 1995, New Britain, Connecticut. Transcript, p. 9.

17. *Ibid.*, p. 12.

18. Patrick Egan, interviewed by the author, September 14, 1995, New Britain, Connecticut. Transcript, p. 4.

19. *Egan.*, p. 12.

20. Dandurand interview, p. 7.

21. *Ibid.*, p. 9.

22. Kornbrekke interview, p. 15.

23. Joseph Jones interview, p. 14.

24. Kornbrekke interview, p. 18.

25. Press release, "The Stanley Works Announces New Business Unit," published by The Stanley Works, July 1995.

26. Richard H. Ayers, interviewed by the author, September 12, 1995, New Britain, Connecticut. Transcript, p. 45.

27. *Ibid.*, p. 52.

28. Robert Hudson, interviewed by the author, October 9, 1995, New Britain, Connecticut. Transcript, p. 9.

29. Ayers interview, p. 66.

30. Stewart Gentsch, interviewed by the author, September 11, 1995, New Britain, Connecticut. Transcript, pp. 12-14.

31. "Stanley's World."

32. Andrew Julien, "Stanley Growing Overseas," *Hartford Courant*, April 20, 1995.

33. Ayers interview, p. 38.

34. Ayers interview, p. 66.

35. Dan Haar, "Stanley to Cut 800 Jobs, 80 in State," *The Hartford Courant*, October 10, 1995, front of the Business section.

36. Patricia McLean, interviewed by the author, New Britain, Connecticut, September 12, 1995. Transcript, p. 42.

37. Ayers interview, p. 56.

38. Hunter interview, p. 25.

39. Ayers interview, p. 68.

40. Hunter interview, p. 28.

41. "Stanley Announces Election of New Officer," Stanley Works press release, September 18, 1995.

42. Hunter, p. 70.

43. *Ibid.*, p. 75.

44. *Ibid.*, p. 76.

45. Ayers interview, p. 42.

46. *Ibid.*, p. 68.

47. "Stanley to Cut 800 Jobs."

48. Press release, "Stanley Announces Initial Phase of Restructuring," October 9, 1995.

49. Huck interview, pp. 32-33.

50. Donna Alexander, interviewed by the author, September 11, 1995, New Britain, Connecticut. Transcript, p. 19.

51. McLean interview, p. 20.

52. *Ibid.*, p. 23.

53. Huck interview, pp. 35-36.

54. Gentsch interview, p. 29.

55. Hunter interview, p. 29.

56. Ayers interview, p. 73.

Appendix

1. "Tool Collectors and Stanley Works," *New Britain Herald*, June 18, 1993.

2. John Walter, interviewed by the author, Marietta, Ohio, September 13, 1995. Transcript, p. 17.

3. John Neary, "When Rules and Drills Drive You Just Plane Screwy," *Smithsonian*, February 1991, p. 56.

4. *Ibid.*, p. 57.

5. Press release, The Stanley Works, October 1980.

6. Walter, interviewed by Torrey Kim, by telephone, March 8, 1995.

7. John Walter, *Antique and Collectible Stanley Tools*, published in 1990 by The Tool Merchant, Marietta, Ohio, p. 3.

8. Walter interview, p. 12.

9. *Ibid.*, pp. 3-9.

10. *Ibid.*, p. 9.

11. *Ibid.*, p. 10.

12. Carl Stoutenberg, interviewed by the author, March 20, 1995. New Britain, Connecticut. Transcript, pp. 6-7.

13. Walter Jacob, interviewed by the author, St. Peters, Pennsylvania, September 14, 1995. Transcript, p. 2.

14. Charles Jacob, interviewed by the author, St. Peters, Pennsylvania, September 14, 1995. Transcript, p. 3.

15. *Ibid.*, p. 11.

16. *Antique and Collectible Stanley Tools*, p. 172.

17. John and Randa Walter, "Charles Miller's 1872 Patent Plow Plane," *Stanley Tool Collector News*, Summer 1995, p. 11.

18. Walter Jacob interview, p. 4.

19. *Ibid.*, p. 6.

20. John Walter, "The First Stanley Tool Collectors Convention," *Stanley Tool Collector News*, Fall 1993.

21. "Tool Collectors and Stanley Works."

INDEX